CONTENTS

PART ONE   PIECES OF THE PAST

1.1	Words from the Past	4
1.2	Pieces of the Past	6
1.3	Secondary Sources	8

PART TWO   BUILDING AN EMPIRE

2.1	Roman Rise to Power	10
2.2	Rivals for Trade	12
2.3	The Roman Army	14
2.4	The Roman Republic	16
2.5	Building an Empire	18
2.6	Julius Caesar	20
2.7	Case Study 1: Caesar Invades Britain	22
2.8	Case Study 2: Claudius Invades Britain	24
2.9	The Emperors	26

PART THREE   LIVING IN THE EMPIRE

3.1	Citizens	28
3.2	Barbarians	30
3.3	The Family	32
3.4	Transport	34
3.5	Trade in the Empire	36
3.6	Roman Towns and Cities	38
3.7	Buildings in Towns and Cities	40
3.8	Living in Towns and Cities	42
3.9	Life in the Countryside	44
3.10	Roman Villas	46
3.11	Religious Beliefs	48
3.12	The First Christians	50

PART FOUR   END OF THE EMPIRE

4.1	The Empire in Crisis	52
4.2	The Collapse of the Empire	54
4.3	The Collapse of the Empire: Gaul	56
4.4	The Collapse of the Empire: Britain	58
4.5	Survival in the East	60
4.6	The Importance of Rome	62
Index		64

1.1 Words from the Past

Historians use **primary sources** to find out about the past. Primary sources come from the time the historian is studying. They become **evidence** when they are used to support a statement. For example, Source A is evidence for the statement that 'Vilbia was a Roman name'. Some primary sources are written down. Many different kinds of written sources have survived from Roman times. For example, words carved on buildings, poems and descriptions of people and places. Some of them are official records and lists of who should pay tax. Some were meant for lots of people to read, others were meant to be kept secret. Often the words were written in Latin. This was the official language of the Roman Empire, although other languages were also used.

A curse written in Latin on a piece of lead. It reads: 'He who stole Vilbia from me, may he waste away like water'.

When an historian reads a primary source, he or she needs to ask certain questions about it:
- When was it written?
- Who wrote it?
- Why was it written?
- Where did the writer get the information from?
- Has it survived as it was written, or has it been copied?
- If it has been copied, could mistakes have been made?

If a number of copies of a written source survive, they can be compared to see if they tell the same story. Sometimes, though, only very few have survived. This makes it harder to be sure that what happened is exactly as it was written.

There are some 'words from the past' in this Unit. They are written primary sources from Roman times.

B

SOURCE

It is impossible for a man to live there for half an hour, but vipers and many snakes and all other kinds of wild beasts live there, and strangest of all, the natives say that if a man crosses the wall he immediately dies, unable to stand the poisonous air. Wild beasts that go there die too!

A description of northern Britain written in the 6th century AD by Procopius.

C

SOURCE

In our orchard I saw you picking
Dewy apples with your mother....
How I saw you!
How I fell in love!

A poem written to a girl by Virgil, a man who lived from 70–19 BC.

THE ROMAN EMPIRE

RARIES

ST J937

Martyn Whittock

Heinemann

Heinemann Library,
an imprint of Heinemann Publishers (Oxford) Ltd,
Halley Court, Jordan Hill, Oxford OX2 8EJ

OXFORD LONDON EDINBURGH MADRID
ATHENS BOLOGNA PARIS MELBOURNE
SYDNEY AUCKLAND SINGAPORE TOKYO
IBADAN NAIROBI HARARE GABORONE
PORTSMOUTH NH (USA)

This edition first published 1994

98 97 96 95 94

10 9 8 7 6 5 4 3 2 1

**British Library Cataloguing in Publication Data is
available from the British Library on request.**

ISBN 0–431–07358–9

Designed by Ron Kamen, Green Door Design Ltd,
Basingstoke

Illustrated by Jeff Edwards Douglas Hall
Stuart Hughes Terry Thomas

Printed in Hong Kong

Acknowledgements

The author and publisher would like to thank the following
for permission to reproduce photographs:
Ancient Art & Architecture Collection: 3.3A, 4.2A
Archäologisches Landesmuseum, Schleswig: 4.1A
Archivio Moro, Rome: 4.6A
Ashmolean Museum: 1.1F
Bibliothèque Nationale: 4.3E
The Trustees of the British Museum: 1.2D, 2.1B, 2.2B, 2.4B,
2.5A, 2.9A, 2.9B, 3.12A, D and E, 4.2C, 4.4A
Simon Chapman: 4.6C
Committee for Aerial Photography, Cambridge: p25
C. M. Dixon: Front cover, 1.2E, 2.1C, 2.3A and C, 2.6E,
3.3C, 3.4B, 3.5B and C, 3.7A, C and D, 3.8A, 3.10A, 3.11A
and C, 4.1C
Sonia Halliday Photographs: 2.2C, 2.4C, 3.5A, 3.8B, 3.8D (F.
H. C. Birch), 4.5A and B
Michael Holford: 1.1A, 1.1D, 3.5B, 3.9C, 3.11D
Israel Museum, Jerusalem: 1.2C
Lion Publishing plc/David Townsend: 1.2A
Mansell Collection: p25
Alan Millard: 1.1E
Museum of London: 4.4F
The National Gallery: 4.6B
National Museum of Ireland: 4.1D
Nationalmuseet, Copenhagen: 3.2G
Dr P. J. Reynolds/Butser Ancient Farm: 3.9D
Rheinisches Landesmuseum, Trier: 3.5A, 3.10B and C
Chris Ridgers: 4.6D
Römisch-Germanisches Museum: 2.9D
Tyne & Wear Museum Service: 3.1D
Vatican Museum: 2.1A

Roger Wood: 3.8C
Woodmansterne Picture Library/Museum of London: 3.9A

We are also grateful to the following for permission to
reproduce copyright material:
Andromeda Oxford Ltd for Source 3.7B, taken from *Atlas of
the Roman World* by Tim Cornell and John Matthews, Phaidon
Press, 1982; B. T. Batsford Ltd for Source 1.2B, taken from
England Before Domesday by Martin Jones; Longman Group
UK Ltd for Source 1.3A, taken from *The Romans in Britain* by
Dorothy Morrison, 1978.

Every effort has been made to contact copyright holders of
material reproduced in this book. Any omissions will be
rectified in subsequent printings if notice is given to the
publisher.

Details of Written Sources

In some sources the wording or sentence structure has been
simplified to ensure that the source is accessible.

The Anglo-Saxon Chronicle (Trans. G. N. Garmonsway), J. M.
Dent and Sons Ltd, 1953: 4.4C
Saint Augustine, *City of God* (Ed. David Knowles), Penguin,
1972: 4.2B
D. Breeze and B. Dobson, *Hadrian's Wall*, Allen Lane, 1976:
2.6B
Julius Caesar, *Commentaries* (Ed. R. L. A. Du Pontet), Oxford
University Press, 1900: 2.7A
Simon Esmonde Cleary, *The Ending of Roman Britain*, Barnes
and Noble Books, 1989: 4.4E
Tim Cornell and John Matthews, *Atlas of the Roman World*,
Phaidon Press, 1982: 2.1D, 2.2A, 2.5B, 3.2F, 3.4C
K. Greene, *Archaeology of the Roman Economy*, Batsford, 1986:
3.4D
Good News Bible, Collins, 1976: 3.1A
Catherine Hills, *Blood of the British from Ice Age to Norman
Conquest*, George Philip in association with Channel 4 TV
company, 1986: 4.3D
J. Liversidge, *Roman Britain*, Longman, 1958: 2.8A
A. Millard, *Discoveries from the Time of Jesus*, Lion, 1990: 2.3B,
2.9E, 3.11B, 3.12B and C
R. W. Moore, *The Roman Commonwealth*, English Universities
Press, 1942: 3.3D
Oxford Dictionary of Quotations, Oxford University Press, 1982:
1.1C
J. Percival, *The Roman Villa: a Historical Introduction*, Batsford,
1976: 4.1B, 4.3B and C
Michael Postan, *The Medieval Economy and Society*, Weidenfeld
and Nicolson, 1972: 4.4G
J. M. Roberts, *History of the World*, Penguin, 1980: 2.6A and C,
4.5C
R. R. Sellman, *Roman Britain*, Methuen, 1956: 2.8B
Diodorus Siculus, *Library of History* (Trans. C. H. Oldfather),
Heinemann, 1939: 2.7B
P. Salway, *Roman Britain*, Oxford University Press, 1981: 2.5E,
2.6D, 2.8C, 2.9CL.
A. Thompson, *Romans and Blacks*, Routledge, 1989: 3.2A, B, C
and E
G. M. Trevelyan, *History of England*, Longman, 1926: 4.4D

SOURCE

A carved stone found on Hadrian's Wall. It dates from about AD 142. It is written in Latin. It reads: 'A detachment of the Twentieth Legion of Valeria and Victrix made this'.

E

SOURCE

Greek writing on a piece of pot from Egypt. It says that a man, named Pekysis, paid his taxes on 12 July, AD 144. He paid 16 silver coins.

F

SOURCE

Writing in a book made from wooden boards. This was found in Egypt and dates from the 1st century AD. It is written in Greek.

Procopius

Procopius (AD 490–570?) was an historian who lived in the eastern part of the Roman Empire, which was often called Byzantium. He was not just an historian, he also wrote about the geography of the lands in and around the Roman Empire.

As well as writing books he was seen as a very good military strategist. He advised the Byzantine military commander in a war against the Persian Empire in AD 527–31.

Procopius also took part in wars against the Vandals in North Africa until AD 536 and against the Goths in Italy until AD 540. These were people who had invaded the lands of the Roman Empire.

As well as writing books about about history and geography, Procopius also wrote books about the building of some of the great Roman buildings. His books included:
- a collection of eight books called *The Wars*
- six books called *The Buildings*
- writings on history nearer his own time, called *The Secret History*.

At times he was able to write from his own experience. At other times he used legends written by other writers about places he had never visited.

1.2 Pieces of the Past

SOURCE

◀ *Remains of a house in Jerusalem. It was burnt in AD 70, when the city was captured by a Roman army.*

Not all primary sources are written down. There are many different types of **non-written** primary sources. Many of these sources have survived from the Roman Empire. Some of them are big, like buildings. Others are small, like coins and tools. They might have been precious objects to the people using them or just ordinary, everyday things. All of these things can tell us about life in the past.

Some sources have been found by accident, others have been carefully searched for. **Archaeologists** are people who study remains from under the ground. They dig into the ground to find these remains. This is called an **excavation**. Here are some different sources which come from the time of the Roman Empire.

C

SOURCE

B

SOURCE

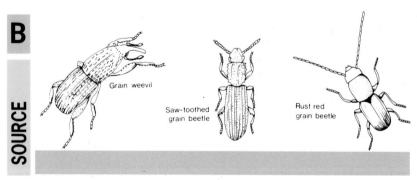

Grain weevil

Saw-toothed grain beetle

Rust red grain beetle

Insects discovered by archaeologists in a Roman building in York, England.

Sandal from Masada, in Israel. From about AD 74.

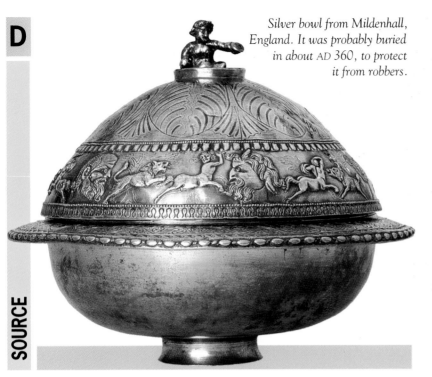

Silver bowl from Mildenhall, England. It was probably buried in about AD 360, to protect it from robbers.

Fiorelli

Giuseppe Fiorelli was the nineteenth century excavator of the ruined Roman city of Pompeii, in Italy, which was destroyed by volcanic erruption in AD 79. The site of this lost city was rediscovered in 1748.

Fiorelli was Professor of Archaeology at Naples. From 1860 onwards he cleared the streets and houses of volcanic ash and pumice to provide a street plan.

Fiorelli divided the city up into districts called **regio** and blocks of houses called **insulae**. This made it possible to identify accurately individual houses. He used plaster to preserve the shapes of people and animals killed and buried in volcanic ash and pumice stone. These can be seen in the Museum at Naples.

◄ *Picture of a woman holding a pen and writing tablet. This is from Pompeii, in Italy. It dates from the 1st century AD.*

1.3 Secondary Sources

Secondary sources usually come from later than the time being studied, and they are always **based on other sources**. Once historians have studied primary sources, they write down what they have learned about the past. What they write down is a secondary source.

Books written by historians do not always agree. Historians may have used different primary sources. They may have understood them differently. You must remember this when you read a history book. These different ways of understanding the sources are called **opinions**. Sometimes the people who wrote the primary sources had different opinions, too. Historians must decide which opinions are best supported by the evidence.

Not all secondary sources are written down. If someone draws a picture of what life was like in Roman times or builds a model of a Roman town, these would also be secondary sources.

The written sources in this Unit tell you about life in Britain before the Romans came, and how it changed when Britain became part of the Empire. They do not all agree with one another! Look at them very carefully.

SOURCE B

Because the Romans were clever and hardworking, and did most things better than the Britons, they soon ruled over all the land.

R. J. Unstead, 'Cavemen to Vikings', 1953.

SOURCE C

The condition of the people improved. Peace brought prosperity, a busy trade sprang up. Along with this corn trade came progress in the mining of tin, lead and copper and the making of weapons and dyeing and pottery.

G. T. Warner and C. Marten, 'Roman Britain', 1923.

An artist's impression of how people lived in Britain before the Romans invaded. From Dorothy Morrison, 'The Romans in Britain', 1978.

SOURCE A

Technically, Roman Britons were able to produce good quality pottery, and a much wider range of iron tools. Farming benefited from the introduction of tools and equipment which enabled more heavily forested land to be cleared.

J. Wacher, 'Roman Britain', 1978.

The tribes of the south-east of England [before the Romans arrived] were skillful farmers, artistic metal workers and well organized. Their rulers must have lived in a degree of comfort. On the whole, the country was peaceful and prosperous.

R. Collingwood, 'Roman Britain', 1923.

For much of rural Britain the Roman invasion of AD 43 meant little change. In Wessex and the South Downs life continued much as before.

S. Woodell, 'The English Landscape', 1985.

By the late Iron Age, lowland Britain was covered with villages, hamlets and farms. This pattern was changed a little during the Roman period but it remained substantially the same. Many Iron Age communities passed unaltered into the Roman period.

T. Rowley, 'Villages in the Landscape', 1987.

Gibbon

Edward Gibbon (1737–94) was a British historian who wrote one of the most famous historical accounts of the Roman Empire. Gibbon was educated at Kingston Grammar School until 1749, then at Westminster School in London. He lived for a time in Switzerland and travelled in France and Italy.

While visiting Italy, Gibbon was inspired to write a history of the fall of Rome. This book, called *Decline and Fall of the Roman Empire*, was published between 1776–88. Gibbon believed that the collapse of Rome had occurred because it was not as morally strong as it had been in the earlier days of the Empire. Gibbon's work tells us as much about his view of the world as it does about the past. He was not sympathetic to Christianity and tried to show that the rise of Christianity was linked to the fall of the Empire.

Characteristics of Gibbon's book:

Part One
This covers Roman history from the second century AD to AD 480.

Part Two
This covers the survival of the Roman Empire in the east from AD 480 to the fifteenth century and the fall of the Eastern (Byzantine) Empire.

Gibbon used more Latin primary sources than Greek ones.

2.1 Roman Rise to Power

According to a Roman legend, the city of Rome was begun in 753 BC. The legend says that its founder was a man named Romulus. He and his brother Remus had been brought up by a wolf! This is a story. Its aim was probably to show how special the city of Rome was. A later legend said that Romulus was the son of Mars, the Roman god of war.

Archaeologists have discovered that, by the 6th century BC, there were a number of important regions in Italy. One of these was Etruria, where the **Etruscan** people lived. They were skilled in metalwork, land drainage, trading, building and road making. An Etruscan (Tarquin II) had made himself King of Rome, a town beside the river Tiber. It was sited at a place where the river could be crossed by a bridge. Ships could also reach Rome from the Mediterranean sea.

In 509 BC, a number of wealthy Roman families forced the king to leave the city. Rome became a **Republic** (a place ruled without a king or a queen). Rome began to grow in importance. Other cities were captured. Their rulers were allowed to keep their power as long as they supplied men for the Roman army and stayed loyal to Rome. This army made Rome strong.

In 390 BC, Rome was attacked and looted by tribes from Gaul (now France). Despite this, the Romans recovered. Then, in three brutal wars, they defeated the tribes from the Italian hills. Between 280 and 275 BC they fought the Greek king, Pyrrhus. He had been helping the Greek settlers, living in Italy, to resist the Romans. By 265 BC, most of southern Italy was controlled by Rome.

SOURCE

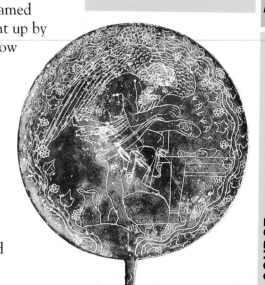

A mirror made by an Etruscan metalworker. It shows a person telling the future by looking at an animal's intestines.

Early Rome and its neighbours

Land controlled by Greek settlers

Invasion by Gauls, 390 BC

GAUL

Etruria
Rome

ITALY

GREECE

Mediterranean Sea

Varro

Varro (116–27 BC) was a writer whose aim was to make Romans aware of their great past. Varro hoped that, if they could be made proud of the past, Romans would act in such a way that their future would be great as well. He had an enormous influence on the thinking of Roman leaders during his lifetime and during the early years of the Roman Empire.

During the civil wars he supported Pompey, the enemy of Julius Caesar. When Pompey was defeated, Varro was pardoned by Caesar. He later became Caesar's librarian and spent his life in study and writing. He wrote while Augustus was Emperor, praising the old-fashioned Roman life of simple morals and worship of the gods of Rome.

Altogether, Varro wrote over 600 books on law, astronomy, geography, history, education and poetry, as well as satires, speeches and letters. His work remained widely read until the end of his life, and even after his death.

2.2 Rivals for Trade

As Rome became more powerful, it was able to control what was bought and sold in Italy. This buying and selling of goods is called **trade**. The Romans found they had **trading rivals**. These were other people who wanted to buy and sell things in Italy. Greek traders had set up cities in Italy and Sicily. Tarentum and Syracuse were two important Greek cities in Italy. Soon they were at war with Rome.

In north Africa there was another great trading city, called **Carthage**. Its people were skilled sailors and shipbuilders. Rome and Carthage were soon rivals. Between 264 and 241 BC the rivalry turned into warfare. The Romans built their first navy to fight the Carthaginian fleet. The Romans captured the island of Sicily and it became the first Roman **province**, in 241 BC. A province was a foreign land captured and ruled by the Romans.

The Carthaginians tried to make up for the loss of Sicily. They captured territory in Spain. From 218–201 BC, a second war was fought with Rome. The Carthaginians were led by a skilled general, **Hannibal**. He led an army across the Alps and into Italy. He defeated the Romans at the Battles of Lake Trasimene and Cannae. Despite this, Rome survived. The towns of central Italy stayed loyal to Rome. The Roman general, Fabius Maximus, avoided any more great battles. Hannibal was not able to capture Rome itself. Soon he was running short of supplies.

The Romans struck back. They attacked the Carthaginian cities in Spain. The Roman army crossed to Africa to threaten Carthage. Hannibal was forced to leave Italy. He went to defend Carthage itself. In 202 BC, he was defeated at the Battle of Zama. In 150 BC a third war broke out. This time the Romans were determined to take no chances. In 146 BC, they totally destroyed the city of Carthage. A new Roman city was built nearby.

A **SOURCE**

The Carthaginians will not injure the people of any other city of the Latins who are subjects [under the control] of Rome. As far as the Latins who are not subjects, they shall keep their hands off their cities, and if they take any such city they shall hand it over to the Romans unharmed. They shall build no forts in Latin territories.

Treaty between Rome and Carthage in 201 BC.

Hannibal

Hannibal (247–183? BC) was the son of Hamilcar Barca, a general of Carthage. Hannibal himself was one of the Carthaginian generals in the Second Punic War. Legends say that he swore to be the eternal enemy of Rome. From 228–183 BC he fought against Rome.

Hannibal was made the commander-in-chief of the armies of Carthage in 221 BC. He married a Spanish princess, and brought her back to Carthage. In 218 BC Hannibal marched into southern Gaul on his way to attack Italy. This is the march on which he used elephants for transport, the action that was praised for its inventiveness, and became one of the most well known facts about Hannibal.

Hannibal marched 750 miles in four months and then crossed the Alps in 15 days. Although he defeated the Romans in several battles he was just not well enough equipped to march on to try to take Rome. He was also forced to rely on local supplies of food because the Romans controlled the sea routes.

After Hannibal was defeated, he managed to escape from the Romans. He eventually took poison rather than be handed over to them.

Roman coin from 125 BC. It celebrates the Roman victory over Carthage, at the battle of Panormus. This battle was fought in 251 BC. In this battle the Romans captured over 100 Carthaginian war elephants.

The site of the Roman city of Carthage.

Trade routes at the time of the wars with Carthage

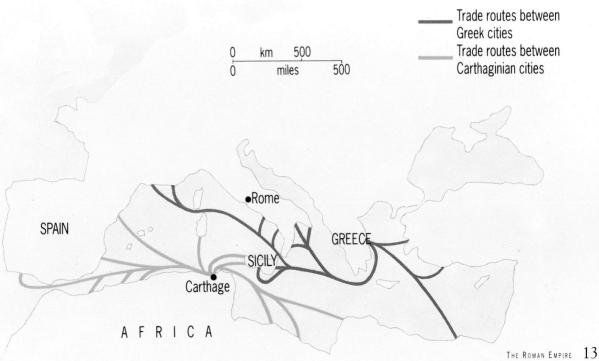

Trade routes between Greek cities

Trade routes between Carthaginian cities

0   km   500
0   miles   500

SPAIN

•Rome

GREECE

SICILY

Carthage

A F R I C A

2.3 The Roman Army

One of the reasons for Rome's success was its army. As Roman power grew, more people were made to join the army. At first the soldiers were the better-off citizens. They copied Greek armies and fought on foot with long spears. To begin with, they were sent home when a war ended. These part-time soliders paid for their own weapons and armour.

As the Roman Empire grew, the army had to fight further away from home. Being a soldier became a full-time job. They were no longer sent home at the end of the fighting. These full-time soldiers were well trained and disciplined. They had to be tough and confident in the use of a number of weapons.

Roman soldiers were grouped into large numbers called **legions**. Each legion was made up of 5,000 heavily armed foot soldiers and some cavalry. The legion included engineers, surveyors, stone masons and carpenters, as well as other craftsmen. As well as fighting major battles, the legions built forts, bridges and roads. When they were on a campaign, they built a camp fortified with banks and ditches at the end of each day's march.

A SOURCE

◀ *Roman legionaries building a fort. The campaigns of the Emperor Trajan (who ruled between AD 98 and 117) are shown on a massive column known as Trajan's Column. This is one of the scenes.*

They trained regularly. At Cawthorne in Yorkshire, they built practice camps where they trained in attacking forts held by the enemy. Only citizens of the Empire could join the legions. They joined for 25 years. When they retired they were given money (three gold coins) and land to farm.

Most of the actual fighting was done by soldiers called **auxiliaries**. They were not citizens of the Empire. They were made citizens when they retired. They included cavalry from Spain and Hungary and archers from the Middle East.

After about AD 100, the Empire stopped growing. The army then spent most of its time keeping hold of the lands that it had captured. This took a lot of men. More and more non-citizens were recruited as auxiliaries to defend the forts on the borders of the Empire.

Tribespeople, from outside the Empire, were also employed. They were put in regiments called **numeri**. Like the auxiliaries, the numeri often defended forts on the frontiers. They were not made citizens when they retired.

D They make a desert and call it 'peace'.

The Roman historian Tacitus, writing in about AD 90. He is describing how the Roman army treated the lands of the enemies of Rome.

Trajan

Trajan (AD 53–117) was the first Roman Emperor who was born outside Italy. He became Emperor in AD 98.

Trajan attempted to enlarge the Empire in the east. He fought wars in Dacia, Arabia, Armenia and Mesopotamia. He was also responsible for building a new aqueduct for Rome. He wanted to be remembered for his victories and as a successful emperor. He had a great column made, carved from stone, which told the story of his Dacian victories.

Trajan was a fair emperor in religious matters. He did not persecute Christians, and was keen to keep law and order.

Trajan's reign seemed settled and secure but already the Empire was beginning to show signs of being under pressure.

◄ *A Roman emperor speaking to his soldiers, as shown on the Arch of Constantine.*

2.4 The Roman Republic

When the last king had been overthrown in 509 BC, Rome became a republic. Power was held by a number of rich families. They met together in the **senate** and were called **senators**. The senate was the main law making group in Rome.

Each year, two senators were elected as **consuls** to run the city. These consuls were elected by a meeting of all the citizens. The voting was arranged so that the rich had more say than the poor in the elections. The consuls were advised by the members of the senate. In an emergency, the two consuls chose one man to be a **dictator** for six months. A dictator had a lot of power. All of these people were men. Women were not allowed to take part.

Other men were elected as **magistrates**. Some helped the consuls. Each year they carried out a census. Some organized sacrifices to the gods of Rome. This kind of government made Rome well organized. However, there was often rivalry between the wealthy families. These families were supported by their followers or **clients**. Rivalry could lead to violence.

Many poorer citizens, called **plebeians**, were not happy. They did not own much land and were often in debt. There was rivalry between the plebeians and the rich members of the senate. In 450 BC, plebeians took action to have Roman laws properly written down. These were called **The Twelve Tables**. The plebeians had two main ways of putting pressure on the wealthy people in Rome. They could refuse to fight in the army and they could threaten to leave Rome and set up their own city. These threats sometimes made the wealthy pay attention to the demands of the plebeians. In 492 BC, some plebeians were appointed as **tribunes**. These men had the power to defend the plebeians from injustice. However, Rome was mainly under the control of the rich. In time, though, some of these were wealthier plebeians.

SOURCE A

The letters 'SPQR' stand for 'Senate and People of Rome'. These letters were put on buildings and on army standards. They helped explain who ran the government of Rome. These letters are from a modern draincover in the city of Rome.

SOURCE B

A Roman copper coin made in AD 23. The letters show that it was made 'By permission of the senate'.

Cicero

Marcus Tullius Cicero (106–43 BC) was a Roman lawyer, scholar and writer who wrote during the civil wars which troubled Rome and which eventually led to the end of the Republic and the start of the Empire. Despite what were seen as its 'failings', Cicero was in favour of the Republic.

Cicero was educated in Rome and Greece. He was forced into exile in 58 BC because his ideas were very unpopular with the powerful leaders in Rome. He was allowed to return in 57 BC, and in 51 BC he became the governor of the Roman province of Cilicia (in modern Turkey).

Cicero opposed Julius Caesar when he became a dictator but was not involved in his murder. Cicero also opposed Octavian (later called Augustus) who eventually ruled Rome as its first Emperor. It was unlikely that any government that was based on a dictatorship would have met with his approval, despite the fact that this system had come about only when the republic disintegrated into squabbling factions and civil war.

Cicero was executed in 43 BC for his criticism of the government.

C

The ruins of the Forum, in Rome. This was a place for debates and legal discussions.

SOURCE

2.5 Building an Empire

After the war with Carthage, Roman power spread. Rome was building an **Empire**. This is when one country conquers and controls other countries. It was not planned out beforehand. As the Romans defeated enemies, they captured many cities and people. More people were brought into the Roman army. Rome could then conquer more land. Every time the Roman army won, it got larger and became more experienced.

Victory also made some important Romans very wealthy. Commanders of armies found that war made them famous. This made them want to fight more wars. After defeating Carthage, Rome turned on Greece. Some Greeks, in Macedonia, had opposed Rome. By 148 BC, Macedonia was beaten. Soon other Greek people came under Roman control. A new province, called Asia, was set up in 133 BC. It included many Greek cities.

Roman armies were soon winning battles from southern France (Gaul) to Egypt. It seemed as if there were no limits to Roman power. Until the Roman army was defeated in Germany, in AD 9, it looked as if nothing could stop the legions.

Each new province added to the Empire was run by a **governor**, who was a member of the senate. The provinces paid taxes to the Roman authorities. With the conquest of Greece, many new ideas spread across the lands under Roman control. For the first time, many different people were being ruled by the same government. Rome was changing peoples' lives.

Countries that were not ruled by the Romans found that it was wise to keep on the right side of them. In this way, Roman power and influence spread far beyond the borders of the lands that they ruled.

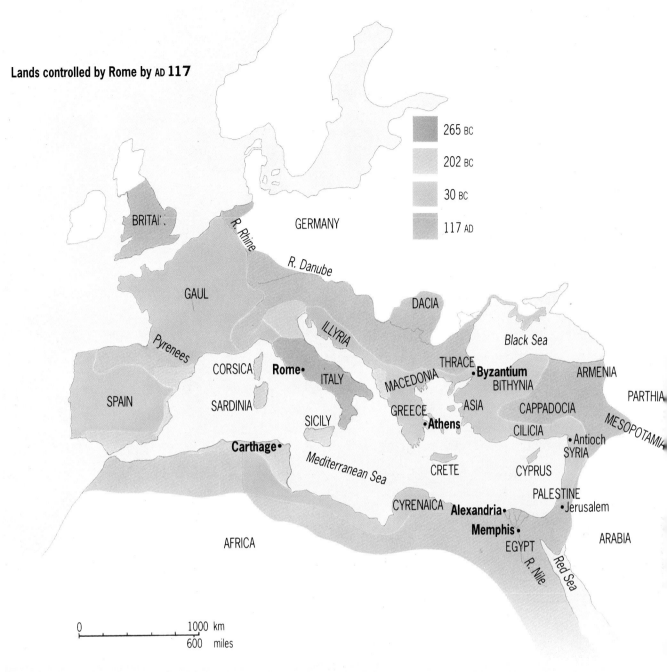

Lands controlled by Rome by AD 117

265 BC
202 BC
30 BC
117 AD

BRITAIN
R. Rhine
GERMANY
R. Danube
GAUL
DACIA
ILLYRIA
Black Sea
Pyrenees
CORSICA **Rome•** ITALY
THRACE **•Byzantium** ARMENIA
MACEDONIA BITHYNIA
PARTHIA
SPAIN
SARDINIA
GREECE ASIA CAPPADOCIA
MESOPOTAMIA
SICILY
•Athens CILICIA
Carthage•
Mediterranean Sea
CRETE CYPRUS
•Antioch
SYRIA
PALESTINE
CYRENAICA **Alexandria•**
•Jerusalem
Memphis•
AFRICA
EGYPT ARABIA
R. Nile Red Sea

0 ——— 1000 km
600 miles

Livy

Titus Livius of Patavium, better know as Livy, (59? BC–AD 17) was one of the three great Roman historians. The other two were Tacitus and Sallust. Livy's history of Rome was a classic in his own lifetime and very popular. He probably started work on the book in 29 BC. He used earlier Roman and Greek histories as the basis for his work. Livy attracted the interest of the first Roman Emperor, Augustus, by his intelligence and original ideas.

Livy was probably not able to use all of the official records when he wrote his book because he was not a member of the government, and access to official records was mainly restricted to these people. He certainly seems less concerned about outline facts. Instead, he concentrated on the personal and moral ideas and actions in Roman history. His *History of Rome from its Foundation* took up 142 books, most of which have been lost.

2.6 Julius Caesar

Despite the victories of Rome over its enemies, there was unrest throughout Italy during the early 1st century BC. Many Italian farmers had been ruined by the wars with Carthage. Many spent long years with the army. The rich treated the poor farmers badly. In Rome itself, the powerful citizens competed for power. The armies were loyal to their commanders, and not to the Roman senate.

Successful generals became very powerful. One, named **Sulla**, returned to Rome as a dictator. He destroyed his enemies and gave their land to his supporters. One of Sulla's supporters was **Pompey**. He defeated pirates who threatened food supplies to Rome. He had won great victories in the Middle East. Some members of the senate opposed Pompey because they were afraid of one man becoming too powerful. Pompey joined with other generals and defeated his enemies in the senate.

One of Pompey's friends was **Julius Caesar**, who became a consul in 59 BC. He led the Roman army in Gaul. Soon he had conquered Gaul. He even led two expeditions to Britain. In Rome, his enemies ordered him home. They feared that he was getting too powerful. As a governor, it was against the law for him to lead his army out of Gaul. He broke this law. He crossed the river Rubicon (the boundary of his province) in 49 BC, and invaded Italy. He faced enemies in Italy, and in the Roman provinces of Spain, Egypt and Africa. His old friend Pompey now tried to control him. Caesar fought back. He chased Pompey to Egypt, where Pompey was murdered. While he was there, Caesar became involved in a civil war that was taking place between the Egyptians. For a short while he was the lover of Cleopatra, the Egyptian Queen. By 45 BC, Caesar had defeated most of his enemies.

Julius Caesar put his friends in places of power in the senate. They elected him dictator for life. He ruled Rome as if he were a king. Many powerful senators were frightened of him. They felt he had too much power, so on 15 March 44 BC, a group of them murdered him.

A SOURCE

There is a story of him [Caesar] joking and playing at dice with some pirates who captured him. One of his jokes was that he would crucify them when he was freed. The pirates laughed, but crucify them he did.

J. M. Roberts, 'History of the World', 1980.

B SOURCE

Caesar would have sought glory and booty [loot] whatever the situation, as part of the normal career of an ambitious nobleman.

B. Dobson, 'Hadrian's Wall', 1976.

C SOURCE

Caesar marched quickly to Spain to defeat seven legions. They were then mildly treated in order to win over as many as possible of the soldiers.

J. M. Roberts, 'History of the World', 1980.

D SOURCE

There is much debate on whether he had a long term plan in life, always intent on supreme power, or was an opportunist. [A person who makes the most of any situation which will help them but does not plan it out in advance.]

P. Salway, 'Roman Britain', 1981.

Some of Julius Caesar's actions.

Gave land to poor citizens.

Reformed the laws.

Ruled like a king.

Built many fine buildings.

Put his friends in powerful positions.

Named a month after himself (July).

Wore purple robes, like a king.

Introduced a new calendar.

Helped many people in Spain and Gaul to become citizens.

Put up his own statue among the statues of the old kings of Rome.

A bust [head and shoulders] of Julius Caesar.

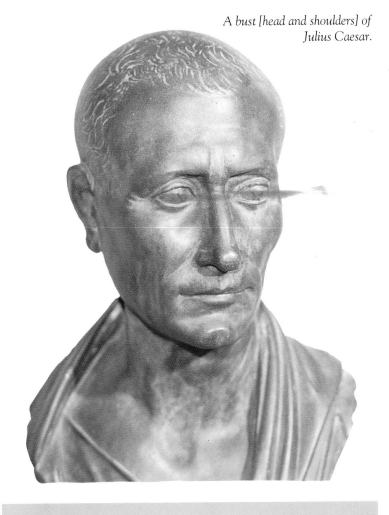

Cleopatra

Cleopatra (69–30 BC) was queen of Egypt. She was also the lover of Julius Caesar and the wife of Mark Antony.

Cleopatra became queen of Egypt in 51 BC, and ruled first with her two brothers, then with her son. She was descended from the Greek general, Ptolomy, and was not Egyptian.

The Romans had been interested in Egypt from 168 BC and Cleopatra tried to win their support to stay in power. After the murder of her lover, Caesar, in 44 BC, she supported his friend, Mark Antony, in the civil wars.

Mark Antony eventually married Cleopatra, in 37 BC, even though this was illegal in Roman law. When Mark Antony was defeated at Actium in 31 BC he committed suicide before Octavian could capture him. Cleopatra tried to win the support of Octavian but failed. She then committed suicide by poisoning herself.

The Roman historian Dio Cassius said about her: *She captivated the two greatest Romans of her day and because of the third, she destroyed herself.*

2.7 Case Study 1: Caesar Invades Britain

In 55 and 54 BC, Julius Caesar led an army to Britain. No Roman general had ever done this before, but this did not mean that the Romans knew nothing about Britain. For many years both Greek and Roman traders had travelled to Britain to buy and sell goods. Also, the Romans had conquered large areas of Gaul (now France) and turned it into a province. In Gaul, the Romans heard many stories about the island of Britain. The Romans also knew that some of their enemies in Gaul were being helped by people from Britain.

When Caesar led his expedition in 55 BC, he came to discover more about Britain and its people. He also came to frighten those British leaders who were helping his enemies in Gaul. A victory would also have made him more famous. Caesar did not bring a large army with him. Bad weather meant that even some of these soldiers were unable to cross the sea.

When Caesar reached Britain he found that the British were armed and ready for him. At first, his soldiers were too frightened to leave their boats. It was only when the standard bearer of the Tenth Legion leapt into the water that the others followed.

Eventually, Caesar's soldiers fought their way ashore. However, four days after he landed, a storm wrecked many of Caesar's ships. He was forced to repair them and take his men back to Gaul.

In 54 BC he came back with a larger army. Marching inland, through modern Kent, he fought a number of battles against the British. Next, he crossed the river Thames. Some of the British went over to the Roman side. In the end, Cassivellaunus, the leader of the British, asked for peace. Caesar took some British hostages, to make sure that their families were friendly towards Rome. He also demanded that the British should pay a sum of money to the Romans every year. Then Caesar returned to Gaul. Britain did not actually become a Roman province until it was invaded again in AD 43.

Two thousand years ago Roman writers disagreed about how worthwhile the invasion of Britain was. In this Unit you will examine some of these primary sources. It is important to remember that one of the reasons why modern historians disagree about what happened in history is because primary sources do not always agree. Each of the sources in the Unit describes Britain.

A **SOURCE**

There is an infinite number of men, very many buildings and very large herds. They use either bronze or gold money. There is timber of every kind.

Julius Caesar writing about Britain. He lived from 100–44 BC.

B **SOURCE**

Their way of life is modest and they are free from the luxuries which come from being rich. The island is thickly populated, much tin is also carried from the British Isles to Gaul.

Diodorus Siculus, writing in about 30 BC.

C **SOURCE**

Britain has gold and silver and other metals. The ocean, too, produces pearls.

The Roman writer Tacitus who lived from AD 56–115.

Twice he [Caesar] crossed the narrow sea and, fighting many battles there, he hurt the enemy more than gained riches for his own men. It was not possible to take anything from people who were poor.

The Roman writer Plutarch who lived from AD 50–125.

He [Caesar] also invaded Britain and defeated the natives from whom he took a large amount of money as well as hostages. Fresh water pearls seem to have been the attraction which led to his invasion.

Suetonius, writing in about AD 120.

The inhabitants of this island refuse money and get what they need by swapping things rather than by buying.

Solinus, writing in about AD 200.

Some suppose that the Britons are named this because they are 'brutes'. They are a people living in the ocean, cut off by the sea. It is as if they were outside the world.

Isidorus Hispalensis, writing in about AD 620.

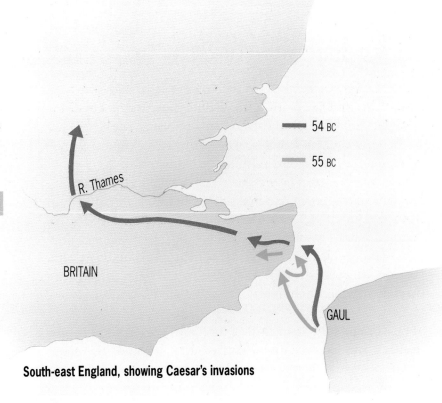

South-east England, showing Caesar's invasions

Cassivelaunus

We do not know when Cassivelaunus was born or died. He was the most powerful British leader in the east and south east of Britain when Julius Caesar invaded in 55 and 54 BC. The centre of his kingdom was the modern county of Hertfordshire; and his main fortress was probably at Wheathampstead.

Caesar, and most other Romans, called Cassivelaunus' tribe the *Catuvellauni*. The British tribes were quite sophisticated, not savage, which is how the Romans often described them. The tribes of the south east of England used gold, silver and, later, copper coins. They had strong trading links with northern Gaul, now France. Many leading warriors from Gaul seem to have escaped to this part of Britain when Caesar conquered large parts of their country. Cassivelaunus had begun to threaten his weaker neighbours – the *Trinovantes* tribe, living in modern Essex and eastern Hertfordshire. The *Trinovantes* asked Caesar for help and he used this as one of his reasons for taking an army to Britain.

In 54 BC, despite Cassivelaunus' use of chariots and his attacks on the Roman army, his fortress at Wheathampstead was captured. He was forced to give hostages to the Romans and promise not to attack the *Trinovantes*. This was soon ignored and the *Trinovantes* were later taken over.

2.8 Case Study 2: Claudius Invades Britain

Julius Caesar visited Britain twice. He fought battles but did not make Britain a province of the Roman Empire. A later emperor, Caligula, planned to make Britain a province of the Empire. He even went as far as bringing a great army to Gaul for the invasion but, at the last minute, he called it off.

In AD 43, **Emperor Claudius** ordered an invasion of Britain. He had been made emperor when Caligula was murdered. Claudius wanted people to think he was a good general. He invaded Britain to prove this. His excuse for the invasion was that a British king friendly to Rome, Verica, had been driven out of his lands by his enemies.

The Roman army landed near Richborough, in what is now Kent. It was led by **Aulus Plautius**. In a great battle, fought at the River Medway, the British were thrown back. When Aulus Plautius reached the Thames, he stopped his advance while he waited for Claudius to arrive from Rome. Claudius was in Britain for sixteen days. During this time, he defeated the British who opposed him in south-east Britain. Their capital, at Colchester, was captured.

Claudius went back to Rome, but the army continued with the conquest of Britain. The Ninth and Fourteenth Legions advanced north and west from Colchester. The Second Legion continued a march along the south coast. Its general, **Vespasian**, captured over twenty British forts, in Hampshire, Dorset and Somerset.

In this Unit you will read different primary sources giving accounts of the invasion. Once again, they do not all tell the same story. You will also read different secondary sources. This will show you how historians use different primary sources and come to different conclusions.

A In AD 43 the Emperor Claudius finally invaded our island with four legions of Roman soldiers. They landed in Kent and marched inland. Some Britons welcomed them, some fought hard against them, but bit by bit they conquered the whole of what we now call England and Wales.

SOURCE

J. Liversidge, 'Roman Britain', 1958.

B The Britons made a valiant effort to defend the line of the river Medway and were only driven off after a fierce two-day battle. Claudius then put in an appearance to claim the victory his subordinate [junior] had already won.

SOURCE

R. Selman, 'Roman Britain', 1956.

C He had received the surrender of eleven British kings, defeated without casualties, and brought barbarian peoples beyond the ocean for the first time under Roman rule.

SOURCE

Inscription in Rome, from the 1st century AD.

D Claudius took the triumph without any effort of his own.

SOURCE

The Jewish historian Josephus, writing in the 1st century AD.

SOURCE E

Having crossed to Britain, Claudius joined the forces which were waiting for him at the Thames. Taking over command, he crossed it and, coming to grips with the forces assembled to oppose him, he defeated them and captured Colchester.

Cassius Dio, who lived from AD 160–230.

SOURCE F

Vespasian fought thirty times with the enemy. He defeated two powerful tribes and captured the Isle of Wight, under the leadership, partly of Aulus Plautius, partly of Claudius himself. Claudius fought no battles and suffered no casualties.

Suetonius Tranquillus, writing in about AD 120.

Claudius

Claudius (10 BC–AD 54) was the nephew of the Emperor Tiberius. The **praetorian guard** (the Emperor's personal bodyguard) made sure that he came to power after the murder of Caligula. The alternative that the Senate was considering at this time was replacing the Emperor with a republic, or at least chosing an Emperor from themselves, rather than from the family that had produced the mentally unstable Tiberius and Caligula.

Claudius was Emperor from AD 41–54. He extended Roman power in North Africa and Britain. He led the successful invasion of Britain himself. However, he was careful to avoid serious wars with the German and Parthian tribes on the frontiers of the Empire.

Claudius enjoyed history, he had been taught by the historian Livy. He wrote several history books, which have not survived. He also improved the legal system. Claudius married four times. He adopted Nero, the son of Agrippina, his last wife, as his heir. Claudius was poisoned, probably by Agrippina. Nero became Emperor.

Maiden Castle, in Dorset. A hill fort attacked by Roman soldiers.

2.9 The Emperors

When Julius Caesar was murdered, in 44 BC, his great nephew **Octavian** came to Rome to take revenge. He had been made Caesar's heir and adopted son. Octavian worked with one of Caesar's supporters – **Mark Anthony** – to destroy Caesar's murderers.

Octavian and Mark Anthony soon quarrelled. At the **Battle of Actium** (31 BC), Mark Anthony was defeated. He and his lover, Cleopatra of Egypt, committed suicide.

Octavian was left in control. Rome had been weakened by twenty years of civil war. He set out to make Rome strong again. He also set about transforming its laws.

In 27 BC, he took the title of **Augustus**. It means 'majestic', or 'noble'. He was now the complete ruler of Rome, although he was careful to show respect to the old Republic. He was also Chief Priest of Rome. Most historians use this date to divide up Roman history. The years before 27 BC they call **The Republic**. The years after they call **The Empire**. From this time onwards, Rome was ruled by emperors. Actually, as we have seen, Rome was building an empire long before 27 BC. Also, Julius Caesar had held as much power as some of the later emperors. However, historians use this date because Augustus set himself up as a more powerful ruler than any other that Rome had known.

When Augustus died in AD 14, power passed to his stepson, Tiberius. Rome was now ruled by a royal family.

A Roman silver coin made in 28 BC. It celebrates the addition of Egypt to the Empire, by Augustus.

A Roman gold coin made in 20 BC. It celebrates the addition of Armenia to the Empire, by Augustus.

Their loyalty was to the family of the emperor, not to the Senate and people.

P. Salway describing the Roman army during the Empire. 'Roman Britain', 1981.

A portrait of the head of Augustus, made of glass. It was probably made soon after his death, in AD 14. However, it makes him appear as if he were a young man.

Caligula

Caligula (AD 12–41) was the nickname of the Emperor Gaius Caesar. It means 'little boots', and it was given to him by the soldiers commanded by his father. Caligula became Emperor in AD 37, following the death of the Emperor Tiberius.

Caligula was a cruel and dangerous man who crushed all forms of opposition to his rule. He was also very ill. In AD 37 he may have become mentally unbalanced as a result of these bouts of illness.

In AD 39–40 he fought in Gaul and seems to have planned an invasion of either Germany or Britain. Neither of these plans came to anything. He returned to Rome. The army brought to the English Channel for an invasion of Britain were used instead to collect sea shells!

Historians think that Caligula may have been planning to marry his sisters in AD 41, a further sign of his growing madness. He was murdered before he could put this plan into effect. His wife and daughter were murdered at the same time.

The army, though, influenced who would be emperor. Tiberius was followed by Caligula, Claudius and Nero. All three were murdered. When Nero was murdered in AD 68, a civil war followed. In AD 69, there were four rival emperors. The war was eventually won in the same year by Vespasian, the general who had fought in Britain.

In AD 192, there was civil war again which lasted until AD 197. Different armies backed different rival emperors. The Empire suffered greatly in these civil wars, as rival generals and nobles fought to become emperor. The emperors became afraid of letting their generals become too powerful and successful. Such a general might try to become emperor himself. As a result, the Empire stopped growing.

Worse than this, the enemies of Rome took advantage of those times when Rome was weakened by civil war.

At home, Augustus improved the state of the country and its people. Abroad, his armies fought battles to win peace through victory. Kings beyond the frontier of the Empire made pacts with him. Ambassadors and princes came from far away with valuable presents: from Persia and India, from Britain and Romania. The senate and people of Rome honoured him for his 'courage, mercy, justice and piety'. His enemies in Rome did not live to tell a different story.

A. Millard, 'Discoveries from the Time of Jesus', 1990.

3.1 Citizens

A **citizen** is a member of a country. As a citizen, a person has certain **rights** and **duties.** A person's rights are those things that they are allowed to do by law. A person's duties are those things that they have to do. Roman citizens had special rights. They could serve in the army, and were protected by the law. They could vote in government elections. They were protected from harsh treatment and certain punishments. They also had duties, such as paying full Roman taxes.

As Roman power spread, the people in some conquered cities were allowed to become citizens. In 91 BC, there was a revolt in Italy. It was led by people who demanded the rights of Roman citizens. It was seen as a good thing to be a citizen.

When the army conquered foreign lands, Roman citizens soon followed. They came as tax collectors, traders and land owners. Ex-soldiers were given land in captured provinces. Cities made up of these citizens were called **colonia**. They often made money out of the natives. Augustus started 75 colonia in foreign lands. They spread the Roman way of life and helped to control and run the Empire. It was also a way to get troublesome people away from Rome! When the leaders of conquered people accepted Roman rule, they were allowed to become citizens. This encouraged them to live and act like Romans.

In AD 212, all free members of the Empire were made citizens. This meant that everyone could be fully taxed.

B **SOURCE**

Gaul is packed with traders, crammed with citizens. No Gaul does business without involving a Roman citizen. Not a penny changes hands without the deal being recorded by a Roman citizen.

The Roman writer Cicero, writing in 74 BC.

C **SOURCE**

What use are laws when money calls all the tunes and people without a gentleman's income have no real rights at all?

The Roman writer Petronius, writing in the 1st century AD. He is talking about poor citizens.

A **SOURCE**

Then the officials tore the clothes off Paul and Silas and ordered them to be whipped. After a severe beating they were thrown into jail. The next morning the Roman authorities sent officers with the order, 'Let these men go'. But Paul said to the officers, 'We were not found guilty of any crime, yet they whipped us in public – and we are Roman citizens. Then they threw us in prison.' The officers reported these words to the Roman officials, and when they heard that Paul and Silas were Roman citizens, they were afraid.

The experiences of two early Christians in the Roman colonia of Philippi (in modern Greece), in about AD 50. It is recorded in the Acts of the Apostles, chapter 16.

ome of the people who were not citizens were **slaves**. A slave
someone who is not free. A slave belongs to a person in the
ay that a horse, or a piece of furniture does. A slave could be
ought and sold and had no rights. However, they were
rotected from the worst treatment by laws passed by the
mperors Augustus and Hadrian. Most slaves were either the
hildren of slaves, or had been captured in wars with the
.oman army.

ome of them were made to do hard work, although others
ere educated. These educated slaves were used as teachers,
nd some became quite powerful servants of the emperors.
ometimes these important slaves were able to buy their own
reedom. Usually, though, slaves only became free if they were
eed by their masters or mistresses. They were then called
reedmen. These freedmen often did important jobs for the
mperor. Some even became wealthy, often as merchants,
uying and selling goods.

Paul

Paul, originally named Saul, of
Tarsus (?–AD 64) was a Jewish
leader born in the Roman Empire
at Tarsus (in modern Turkey).
Saul was a Roman citizen. He
joined in the persecution of the
early Christians. Later he
became a Christian himself, after
seeing a vision of Jesus while he
was travelling on the road to
Damascus. This was when he
changed his name to Paul.

After a time of study and prayer
in Arabia he returned to
Damascus and then moved on to
Jerusalem. Later he travelled
great distances preaching about
Jesus, mostly to the non-Jewish
people of Asia Minor and
Macedonia.

Paul set up many Christian
communities, and wrote many
letters explaining about the
Christian faith. He was finally
executed, in Rome, on the
orders of the Emperor Nero.
He was later made a saint.

*Tombstone of a woman named Regina
who was a British slave. She was bought
by a soldier who freed her and married
her.*

3.2 Barbarians

People who lived outside the Empire were known as **barbarians**. This is a Greek word, used to show that they did not speak a respected language. Respected languages were Greek, and then Latin. These were the main languages of the Empire.

Barbarians did not live, dress, or speak like Roman citizens. Romans often thought of them as uncivilized savages. In reality, they had their own ways of life. The barbarians were very attracted to the wealth of the Empire, and often hoped to share in it. Some, especially towards the end of the Roman Empire, served as soldiers in the Roman army. Others raided the lands of the Empire, to steal. Some barbarians tried to settle inside the Empire and live like Romans. As Rome grew weak, the powerful barbarian peoples became a threat to the Empire.

The Romans had mixed views of the barbarians. Often they looked down on them. At other times they were willing to use them if they could. Some Romans even found it fashionable to copy attractive characteristics of barbarian people. The sources in this Unit will show you some of these mixed views.

A SOURCE

Too tall. Lank blond, or red hair. Light blue eyes. Upturned noses. Huge bellies. Simple minds. Quick tempers. Brave. Reckless. Drunken. Lazy. Gambling and boastful.

A modern historian's list of Roman descriptions of northern barbarians. From L. A. Thompson, 'Romans and Blacks', 1989.

B SOURCE

Pale brown faces. Straight nose. Bright brown eyes. Brown hair. Thin lips. Not too tall.

A modern historian's list of Roman descriptions of perfect appearance. From L. A. Thompson, 'Romans and Blacks', 1989.

C SOURCE

We change our hair colour to blond, because men find us more attractive that way.

The Roman poet Martial on how Roman women copied barbarian looks. Written in the 1st century AD.

D SOURCE

Africans have whiter souls than the whitest of Greeks.

Roman comment, from about AD 250.

The kingdom of Ethiopia is a fertile and rich wonderland, possessing an abundance of gold and a royal family descended from the gods.

From a Roman geography book written in about AD 250.

In 151 BC Sulpicius Galga, who had massacred thousands of Lusitanians [from modern Portugal] after they had surrendered to him, was acquitted [found not guilty] at his trial. Very few people in Rome cared much about what happened to the Barbarians.

T. Cornell and J. Matthews, 'Atlas of the Roman World', 1982.

Roman gold and silver coins, found in the village of Ginderup, in Denmark. These coins were probably buried in about AD 100.

The people who lived in Ginderup were not members of the Roman Empire. They lived far beyond its frontiers. Archaeologists believe that the coins probably belonged to a barbarian tribesman who served in the Roman army. He may have buried the coins, for safety, when he returned to his native village.

Tacitus

Cornelius Tacitus (AD 56–?) was one of the three greatest Roman historians. We know very little about his early life. He probably came from southern France or northern Italy. His father may have been an administrator in Trier or Cologne. He lived most of his life during Emperor Trajan's reign, though he may have lived a few years into the reign of the Emperor Hadrian. We know that he was probably a governor of a military province and was a proconsul in Asia from AD 112–13. He married the daughter of the successful general, Agricola, in AD 77.

Tacitus gave a clear account of the campaigns fought by his father-in-law in his *Life of Agricola*. This tells about the campaigns fought in Britain by the Roman army. *The Histories* give a detailed account of Roman history between AD 14–96 and are very favourable to the Emperor Vespasian. In the *Annals* he complained about the morals of other Emperors. In the *Germania* he wrote about the German tribes who lived north of the rivers Rhine and Danube.

Tacitus used old sources of information to write the *Germania*; it was out of date even when he wrote it. He described the Germans as unspoiled by the corruption which had, in his opinion, spread across the Empire.

3.3 The Family

The family was very important to the Romans. Each family was under the control of the father. In Latin, he was called the **paterfamilias** (the father of the family). He had complete control over all relatives and servants in the house. His sons stayed under his control until he died.

The paterfamilias led the family in its worship of the gods. It was believed that household gods looked after each family.

Related families were grouped together and shared a name. A group of related families was known as a **gens**. Each member of the gens had his or her personal name and the name of the gens. This showed which group of families they belonged to.

Women were under the control of their husbands or fathers. However, they controlled how the house was run. The Roman mother was called the **materfamilias** (mother of the family).

Some women tried to be more independent and educated. Roman writers were not always happy with this. They felt a woman's place was running the home.

This is how families were organized in Rome. However, we must remember that the Roman Empire was very large. There were some groups of people living within the Empire who organized themselves differently. For example, in Britain during the 1st century AD there were women who were very powerful rulers. One, named Boudicca, ruled a tribe called the Iceni. Another, named Cartimandua, ruled a tribe called the Brigantes.

The Roman writer Cato, who lived from 234–149 BC.

A

SOURCE

Statues of a family from Palmira, in modern Syria. They are members of the Roman Empire but are dressed in middle-eastern clothes from the 2nd century AD. These people would have spoken the Palmirene language instead of Latin. They would have followed Arab ways of life, not Roman ones.

Bathing a baby. A carving from Rome.

Boudicca

Boudicca (?–AD 62) was the wife of Prasutagus, ruler of the Iceni tribe in East Anglia, Britain. When Prasutagus died, in AD 60, much of Britain was under Roman rule. His kingdom was independent, but he was only allowed to rule as an ally of Rome. Prasutagus left his kingdom to the Emperor and his own daughters. He did this in the hope that the Emperor would let his family continue to rule. He was wrong, possibly because the Romans did not think women should rule a tribe.

Roman government officials took over the kingdom. When there were protests, Boudicca was badly beaten and her daughters were raped. In response, Boudicca led her people in a revolt against the Romans. She was helped by the *Trinovantes* tribe from Essex. Many of them had lost land to Roman settlers around the new Roman city of Camulodunum (now Colchester).

Boudicca's army destroyed the new Roman towns of Camulodunum, Verulanium (St Albans, Hertfordshire) and Londinium (London). The towns were burned and the inhabitants massacred. The main Roman army was away fighting in North Wales and was unable to prevent the destruction. Eventually the governor, Suetoneus Paulinus, defeated Boudicca. She committed suicide.

D

You were a faithful wife to me, and an obedient one. You were kind, gracious and friendly. You worked hard at your spinning. You did not dress so as to be noticed, nor did you show off your running of the house. You did your duty to the household. You tended my mother as if she had been your own.

A Roman description of a faithful wife from the 1st century BC.

3.4 Transport

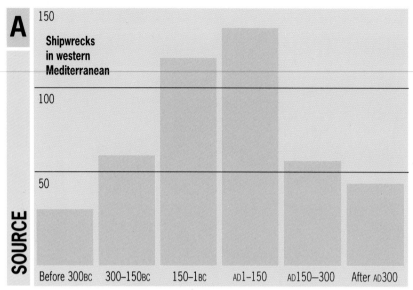

Shipwrecks in western Mediterranean

150

100

50

Before 300BC | 300–150BC | 150–1BC | AD1–150 | AD150–300 | After AD300

SOURCE

This graph shows the number of ancient ships found by underwater archaeologists, in the western Mediterranean.

C

The roads were carried straight across the countryside, were paved with cut stones and supported underneath with masses of tightly-packed gravel. Hollows were filled in and ravines that cut across the route were bridged.

SOURCE

Plutarch, who lived from AD 50–120, describing roads built by the army.

The Roman Empire needed good transport routes. The army had to move about quickly. Food had to be carried to Rome. Taxes had to be collected. The evidence which has survived about Roman transport shows us just how important it was. There were four main forms of transport: by road; by sea; by river; by canal. Many clues remain about each sort.

▼ *Painting of a Roman ship from Ostia, near Rome. The ship was called the 'Isis Giminiana'. The captain's name was Farnaces.*

B

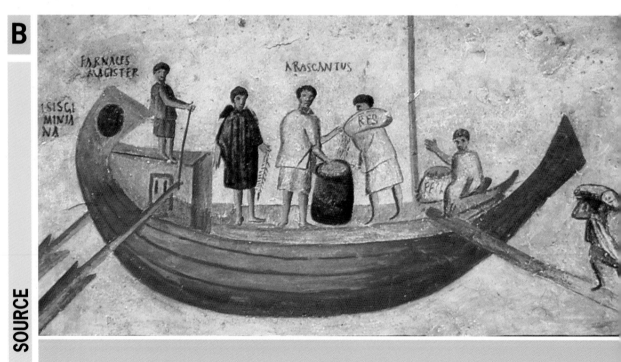

SOURCE

I think I should bring to your attention any plan which is worthy of your immortal name and glory. There is a large lake, near Nicomedia, across which marble, food, and timber for building are easily brought by boat as far as the main road.

After this everything has to be taken to the sea by cart, with great difficulty and increased cost. To connect the lake with the sea would require a lot of workmen but there are plenty of them available.

◀ *Letter from Pliny, Governor of Bythinia, in modern Turkey, to the Emperor Trajan, in about AD 112. He is writing about a plan for a new canal.*

Thousands of miles of Roman roads survive to be studied. They were so well made, that archaeologists can tell that a lot of effort went into building them. We also know about the roads from other sources of evidence. Some of these sources are descriptions of how the roads were made. Some are descriptions of the best way to get from one place to another, and the distance between the places. These sources are called **itineraries**. Several have survived from Roman times. One, called the **Peutinger Table**, is a map of the world known to the Romans. It shows towns and roads. Another, called the **Antonine Itinerary**, lists 225 routes around the Empire and the distance between places.

Other forms of evidence, like the **Acts of the Apostles** in the New Testament, show us that people were able to travel around fairly easily. We also know that the Romans travelled by sea. There are mosaics and paintings of ships. These show us what Roman boats looked like. Official documents have survived. These tell us that thousands of tons of grain were carried, by ship, from north Africa to Rome. Underwater archaeologists have even found the remains of Roman ships. Some of these sank at sea. Others sank in rivers and harbours. Roman ships have been found in the river Thames, near the Roman port of Londinium (London). One, found at Madrague de Giens, off the south coast of France, was carrying wine and fine pottery.

The Romans also dug man-made rivers. These are called **canals**. The rivers Rhine and Meuse (in Germany) were linked by a canal. Another canal called the Car Dyke carried goods in eastern England. As well as these surviving canals, we also have evidence in Roman documents, explaining why canals were useful. All of these surviving primary sources give us information about the importance of travel in the Empire.

Plutarch

Plutarch (AD 50–120) was a philosopher and biographer. He was born at Boeotia, in central Greece, but visited Athens, Egypt and Italy. He lectured and taught in Rome. He was a supporter of the traditional religious beliefs of Greece and Rome and became a priest at the famous shrine at Delphi in Greece.

Plutarch believed that the learning and education of Greek culture should be united with Roman power for the good of the Empire. He often advised the performing of small duties and responsibilities as important: *Leave the Battle of Marathon and past glories to the schools of rhetoric,* was his advice to those in power. His ideas were thought to be important by many people involved in governing of Rome.

Plutarch wrote books on politics, philosophy and religious beliefs. He also wrote about the lives of several emperors, and other famous people of the time, including Cicero.

3.5 Trade in the Empire

The Roman Empire was very good for trade, for a number of reasons. The large Roman army needed to be supplied with food, clothes, pottery and weapons. Soldiers and other people who worked for the government were paid with coins. They wanted to buy things with their money.

The Romans brought peace to many countries. This was called the **Pax Romana**. It made it safe to travel long distances. Good roads helped as well. Roman towns were useful places in which people could meet to buy and sell goods.

Most trade began with supplying the army with what it needed. Roman merchants organized this. They also helped the government to buy grain to feed the people living in Rome. These merchants were called **negotiatores**. They bought things like wine, food and pottery and transported them to the army.

The negotiatores began to see that they could sell things to ordinary people, too. Soon they were carrying these things on the ships loaded with army supplies. Expensive pottery and glass could be carried on ships loaded with olive oil, wine or grain. The pottery or glass took up only a little space. However, it could be sold for high prices. Pottery from Italy and Africa was carried as far as Germany, Britain and the province of Gaul.

A carving of a Roman ship carrying wine barrels.

A

SOURCE

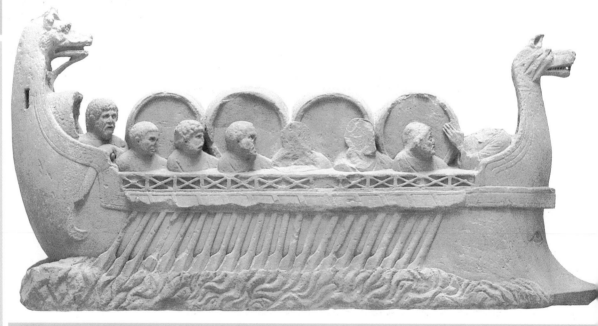

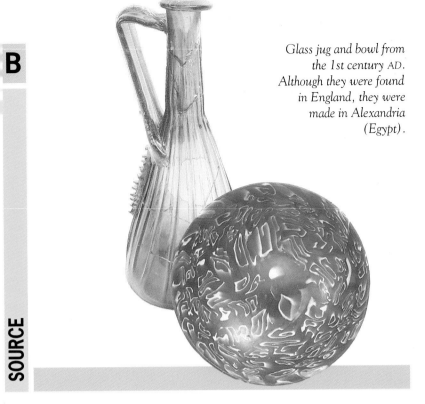

Glass jug and bowl from the 1st century AD. Although they were found in England, they were made in Alexandria (Egypt).

Cunliffe

Barry Cunliffe is a modern-day archaeologist. He has excavated a number of important Roman sites in Britain including Bath, Danebury hillfort, Fishbourne, Hengistbury and Portchester.

In 1979 Cunliffe began a detailed study of Hengistbury Head, Dorset. This headland, which faces the Solent, was an important trading port from about 100 BC. To make it easier to reach the port, the Romans had a deep water channel dug. Valuable items were brought in from the Roman world and areas influenced by Rome.

These goods included figs, Italian wine, fine pottery from Armorica (part of modern France) and expensive glass. They were probably brought to Britain by Roman merchants. The merchants would have traded them for goods Britain produced that Rome needed: metals, hides and corn; possibly slaves and hunting dogs too.

Many craftsmen and women found they could sell their goods to more people than ever before. In the town of Lyons (in Roman Gaul), negotiatores put together loads of goods to be taken as far away as Britain and the rivers Rhine and Danube.

Not all the trade was carried out by rich negotiatores. All over the Empire, farmers, potters and metal workers saw a chance to make more money. They sold their goods at local towns and markets.

C

Sunken grain storage jars. From Ostia, the port of Rome.

3.6 Roman Towns and Cities

The Romans are famous for their **towns** and **cities**. The Romans did not invent them. People around the Mediterranean had lived in towns for many centuries. What the Romans did was make them bigger than ever before, and build them in places which had never had towns before. The people who lived in the biggest Roman towns were given the right to run them. We call these very large towns, cities. Even after hundreds of years the ruins of cities survive, when other kinds of evidence decays. This helps to explain why people think of towns when they think of the Romans.

The larger Roman towns were usually carefully planned. They had a meeting place called the **forum**. Government officials often had their own building, called the **basilica**. From here they could control the running of the town and the land around it. Some large towns, like Calleva (Silchester), in England, were originally less carefully planned. But as people became more like their new Roman rulers they copied the Roman ways of planning towns. Smaller towns were never well planned. They had few big buildings.

▶ *The walls of many towns were improved in the 4th century AD. New towers were added, which stood out from the walls. They made it harder for enemies to attack the town. The ditches around the towns were also redug.*

and they were all the same in any part of the Empire

SOURCE

A *The walls and towers of the Roman city of Constantinople, in modern Turkey. Walls were built around towns and cities to keep them safe from attack. These walls and towers were built in about AD 413.*

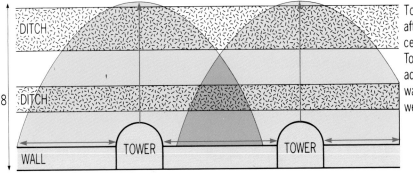

Town defences after the 4th century AD. Towers were added to the walls. Ditches were redug.

☐ Area reached by weapons fired from the walls.

//// Area in front of walls, out of reach of defenders weapons.

⟶ Direction and distance weapons could be fired from town walls.

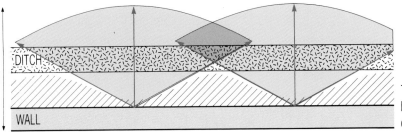

Town defences before the 4th century AD.

The Roman government controlled the new provinces through towns and cities. People came to towns to pay taxes. In order to pay their taxes, they sold what they had grown, or made, for Roman coins. Any money left after they had paid their taxes could be spent in the towns. This encouraged other people to bring their goods to town, to sell for cash. Roman taxes gave life to the towns. When the taxes stopped, people stopped buying and selling and the towns came to an end.

Constantine

The Emperor Constantine (?–AD 337) was responsible for the building of a new Roman city. He founded it on the site of an old town named Byzantium but his new city was to be a 'new Rome' and was called Constantinople (in modern Turkey).

The new city was to be near the eastern frontiers of the Empire. Work started in AD 326 and the city was **dedicated** (formally opened with sacrifices for the god who the Romans wanted to look after the town or city) in AD 330, with both pagan and Christian ceremonies. It copied many of the buildings of Rome but without the pagan temples; Constantine was in favour of Christianity.

B

A gold coin. This one shows the Emperor Antonius Pius, who was emperor between AD 138 and 161. It would have been worth more than a small farmer earned in one year. Taxes had to be paid in gold and silver coins.

SOURCE

3.7 Buildings in Towns and Cities

Carving showing a Roman shop.

The remains of Roman towns show some of the skills used by Roman planners and builders. A person who plans how a building should be built is called an **architect**. Roman architects planned fine buildings with great **arches** and **domes**. Roman builders invented **concrete**. This is a mixture of water, sand, stone and cement. Concrete helped to make the buildings strong.

Government buildings were made out of fine stone and paid for with money raised in taxes. Marble is a beautiful stone and the government controlled its supply. This was a way of making money, and making sure there was enough marble for government buildings.

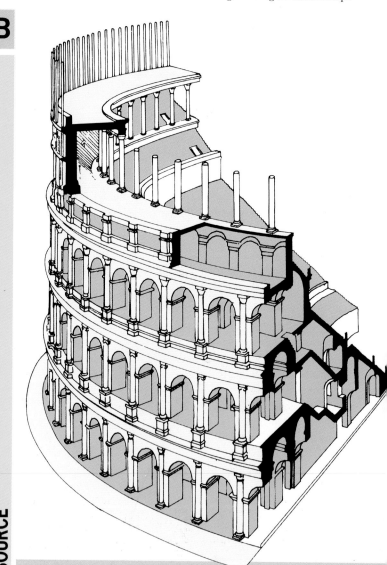

A modern drawing which shows Roman building skills. The weight of the whole building is carried by the arches. This downward force is spread sideways by the arches. A complete circle of arches stops this sideways force from breaking the arches apart.

SOURCE

C

◀ *The Roman baths at the city of Aqua Sulis (Bath) England. Everything above the square bases of the pillars is a Victorian reconstruction of what the baths might have looked like. It is not Roman, it was made in the 19th century AD.*

Most buildings were made from whatever local stone was available. Others were made from wood and tiles. In the Middle East mud bricks were used for building.

As well as fine buildings, towns contained lots of shops. In this Unit you will find examples of the kinds of building skills and shops found in Roman towns.

D

Vespasian

Vespasian (?–AD 79) was a successful military commander. He held the rank of legate in the II Legion Augusta during the invasion of Britain.

In AD 63 Vespasian became proconsul of Africa. In AD 67 he fought in the Middle East. When the Emperor Otho died in AD 69, Vespasian was proclaimed Emperor by the legions in the Middle East.

Vespasian was responsible for many building projects in Rome. He restored the Capitol and built a new Forum. He built a Temple of Peace and started building the Colosseum, a huge arena, in AD 70–72.

The Colosseum was dedicated by Vespasian's son, Titus, in AD 80. It was finished by his other son, Domitian, in AD 82. The Colosseum was built with stone and concrete and could seat 50,000 people.

◀ *Carving showing a Roman shop.*

3.8 Living in Towns and Cities

◀ *Public toilets in the Roman town of Thugga (Tunisia) in north Africa.*

By AD 1, over one million people lived in Rome. The majority lived in blocks of flats, called **insulae**. The poorer Romans rented these flats.

The flats were badly built. They had no heating or running water. People could be turned out of their rooms by their landlords. Buildings often collapsed, or caught fire.

There were sewers under the streets, but only the houses of the rich were able to use them. Poorer people were tempted to dump their rubbish in the street, or in the river Tiber. Streets were filthy, dark and dangerous, and disease was common.

▼ *A Roman aqueduct, in Tunisia. An aqueduct carries water from one place to another. This aqueduct carried water 60 miles to the Roman city of Carthage. It was built between AD 117 and 138.*

B

ɡladiators fighting animals and a prisoner being fed to a leopard. This mosaic is ɾom Zliten, in modern Libya, north Africa.

Many poorer citizens were unhappy with their lives. So owerful leaders would put on great entertainments to try to ɛeep them happy, or to win their support. Wealthy people night pay for a chariot team. Fierce support for a team could ɛad to riots. Another popular entertainment was watching ɦen and women fight to the death. These people were known ɪs **gladiators**. Also, many people went to the theatre to watch ɬlays being performed.

Spartacus

Spartacus was one of the many gladiators who fought regularly to entertain the crowds in Roman cities. He came from Thrace, in Greece. In 73 BC he led a huge, and initially successful, slave revolt in southern Italy.

Spartacus and his men defeated two Roman armies, and laid waste to southern Italy. At its biggest, Spartacus' army may well have had 90,000 men. In 72 BC they defeated another three Roman armies and marched through northern Italy. Spartacus planned to end the war there and go home. His men wanted to fight on. In 71 BC they were defeated by the Roman general Crassus. All his men who were captured were crucified. Spartacus was killed in battle.

Theatre in the city of Ephesus, in modern Turkey. It was built between 250 and 150 BC. It was altered in the 1st century AD.

3.9 Life in the Countryside

Most people living in the Roman Empire did not live in large cities and towns. They lived in the countryside where there were smaller towns, villages, groups of farms and single farms. Most people in the Empire worked on the land.

Most rich Romans owned large areas of land, called **estates**. Estates were scattered all over the Empire. In the 4th century AD, a wealthy woman named Melania owned land in Italy, Sicily, Africa, Spain and Britain. Many of the people farming the land would have been tenants of a rich landowner like Melania. These tenants did not own the land, they rented it. Some poorer farmers worked on the landowner's land without pay, as a form of rent.

The Empire covered areas with very different climates and different types of farming. In all areas, most of the land was divided into estates. From as far apart as Gaul (modern France) and modern Bulgaria there is evidence that villages of tenants lay nearby the great houses of the landowners. Sometimes the landowner employed a manager who lived in the great house and ran the estate.

Although they were altered over the years, their basic plan did not change. A door led from the street into a paved courtyard and various rooms opened from that. Stone pillars helped to hold up the flat roof and there were stone steps to climb up on to the roof.

A modern archaeologist's description of village houses in the Middle East during the Roman Empire.

A modern reconstruction of a dining room in a Roman country house, in about AD 350.

Many of the farms and villages changed little during the time they were ruled by Rome. Here and there, though, a better off farmer might copy Roman fashions. These 'Roman farms' often had tiled roofs, painted plaster walls, mosaic floors and central heating. Other farmers bought pottery, tools and brooches. When archaeologists find lots of Roman pottery on the site of a farm, they know that the people who lived there were making the most of Roman trade. They were growing more crops and looking after more animals than they needed in order to feed themselves. They sold any extra, or **surplus**, food and animals in order to get money to pay their taxes. But they also managed to buy things for themselves – most people could afford at least to buy some Roman-style pottery.

Columella

Columella was born in the early part of the first century AD, in Spain. He fought as a **tribune** in the VI Legion in AD 36 in Syria.

Columella was not just a soldier. He also had estates in central Italy. He was not simply interested in owning land, or in the money that land could make – he also took a keen interest in agriculture. He liked to think of ways to improve the traditional ways of farming to make it more productive.

Between AD 60–65 he wrote about farming in twelve books entitled *The Countryside*. In his books he gave advice on farm buildings, farm workers, different types of soil, different crops including vines, olives and fruit, and looking after farm animals and fishponds.

Columella believed that estates should be carefully managed. He felt that farming in Italy had declined and needed landowners who would take a personal interest in the running of their estates. His books were widely read and influenced the thinking of many Roman landowners.

C

Roman mosaic from Tunisia. It shows a thatched house from Roman north Africa.

D

◄ *A modern reconstruction of a farmhouse from Hampshire in England. Many poorer farmers would have lived in houses like this, in Roman Britain.*

3.10 Roman Villas

Villa is a Latin word which means both 'house in the countryside' and 'farm'. Historians and archaeologists disagree about exactly which buildings should be called villas. Some think that farms in towns should be called villas, but most insist that a villa must be in the countryside. Some say that any grand house in the countryside should be called a villa, but most think that a villa should be at the centre of a farm or large estate. All agree that villas must be **romanized** buildings, not farms built in the native style.

Some villas were huge luxury houses. They had wide corridors, rectangular rooms, bath houses and underfloor heating called a **hypocaust**. They usually had barns and other outbuildings for farming. The actual work on the farm would be done by slaves or peasants, who would live somewhere else on the estate.

▼ *A wall painting from Trier. This dates from about AD 150. It is a Roman artist's impression of a villa, with its workers.*

A

SOURCE

The first villas were built in Italy. Many of these were huge houses, run by slaves. As the Roman Empire grew, native people began to copy the Romans and build villas themselves. In northern Gaul, the countryside was full of villas by the end of the Empire. As people became more successful in agriculture, so more villas were built. In north Africa the land was carefully watered (**irrigated**) in order to produce more crops. As they produced more crops, farmers became more wealthy and spent much of their money on rebuilding their homes as villas.

Villas were expensive to build and maintain. For instance, they needed skilled workers from the towns to make things like mosaics. If people were to carry on living in villas, and to build new ones, the Empire needed to be peaceful and prosperous. If the countryside was raided too often, or if trade was reduced, there would not be enough skilled workers, or enough money, to build more villas.

A bronze statue from Trier in modern Germany. It shows a villa ploughman in his outdoor clothes.

A mosaic of a Roman villa from north Africa. It shows the villa buildings and some of the life of the villa. It dates from about AD 320.

Cogidubnus

Cogidubnus (?–AD 75) was king of the Atrebates tribe on the south coast of Britain from about AD 43, his kingdom centred on Chichester. He is mentioned by Tacitus as being loyal to Rome. The Romans increased his power; his kingdom became an ally of the new Roman government in Britain. He was probably made a senator by Claudius in AD 47.

The Roman-style villa at Fishbourne, Sussex, which has huge buildings, mosaics and gardens, was probably built as his palace.

3.11 Religious Beliefs

Within the Roman Empire, people believed in many different gods and goddesses. The most important Roman god was Jupiter. There were large temples of Jupiter on the Capitoline hill in Rome, at Doliche in Turkey, and at Baalbek in Syria. Other Roman gods and goddesses included: Neptune, the sea god; Juno, the wife of Jupiter; Mercury, the messenger of the gods; Mars, the war god; Venus, the goddess of love and Minerva, the goddess of wisdom and war.

After Emperor Augustus died in AD 14, emperors themselves began to be worshipped as gods. The emperor was the Chief Priest of the gods. Great services were carried out to please the gods. Animals were sacrificed to the gods of Rome. The government organized and led this worship of the gods.

Many Roman beliefs were based on Greek religious beliefs. Most of these beliefs involved carrying out sacrifices to please the gods. Religious beliefs did not ask people to live good lives. Neither did religion offer people a personal relationship with a god.

B SOURCE

Emperor's order: It is my will that graves and tombs lie undisturbed forever. Respect for those who are dead is most important: no one should disturb them in any way at all. If anyone does, I command that he be executed for tomb robbery.

An order of the Emperor, from the 1st century AD. It was found in Nazareth in modern Israel.

The Temple of the Roman god Jupiter, in the Roman city of Thugga, in modern Tunisia. It was built in the centre of the city for all to see in AD 166.

A SOURCE

Underground temple of the 'mystery' god Mithras in Rome.

People throughout the Empire had their own gods and goddesses. They were free to worship them as long as they also worshipped the gods of Rome. Local people often linked their god to the Roman god most similar in character. At Trier (in Germany) the local god Lenus was renamed Mars-Lenus. At Bath (in England) the local god Sul was renamed Sul-Minerva.

By the 2nd century AD, Roman citizens began to be interested in gods from the east of the Empire. One man, Apollonius, travelled to India to find out about other religions. People began to worship Eygptian goddesses like Attis and Cybele. The Persian god Mithras was popular among soldiers. These new religions were called **mystery religions**. People had to pass secret tests to become members of the mystery religions.

A carved head from Bath, England. It is probably the British god, Sul. In this carving the god is made to look like the Roman goddess, Minerva.

Apollonius

Apollonius of Tyana was a wandering philosopher and teacher. He was born in the early first century AD at Tyana in modern Turkey. He travelled to India to discover other religions.

Apollonius was threatened with death by both the Emperor Nero and the Emperor Domitian for his beliefs. Little is known about these beliefs, as only a few scraps of his writing have survived.

Apollonius is mentioned by Philostratus in AD 200, but he is seldom used as a source by modern historians as he is regarded as unreliable.

3.12 The First Christians

In about AD 33, the Jewish preacher and teacher Jesus was executed by the Roman governor Pontius Pilate. Soon the friends of Jesus were spreading the news that God had raised him from the dead. The followers of Jesus' teachings were called **Christians**. Christianity promised people a new relationship with God, instructions on how to live a good life, and life after death. It grew in popularity, often among the poorer citizens. By the 2nd century AD, Christians were being punished by the Roman authorities. This was because they refused to worship the official gods of Rome. Many had already been killed by the Emperor Nero.

Some people distrusted the new religion. They did not understand what Christians believed. At Smyrna (in modern Turkey) and Lyons (in modern France) Christians were killed by mobs. The mobs could kill Christians because Roman law did not protect their religion.

Despite these problems, Christianity continued to attract people. Some emperors allowed it to continue. Others punished the followers of Jesus. However, many people were impressed by the brave way in which Christians stood up to punishment.

A

SOURCE

Early Christians praying in the 4th century AD. From a chapel in the villa at Lullingstone, England.

Painting of the head of Jesus from the villa at Hinton St Mary, England. It dates from the 4th century AD. The letters behind the head are a Christian sign. They stand for: 'Jesus Christ'.

Theodosius I

Theodosius I (AD 346–95), is also known as Theodosius the Great. He was a Christian Emperor who was committed to the idea of spreading Christianity among as many people as possible.

Theodosius fought against the barbarian Goths in AD 378 and became Emperor of the eastern Empire in AD 379. He also fought against the barbarian Visigoths.

Theodosius was determined to defend the church against any beliefs which he felt were wrong. He even brought in the death penalty for members of extreme religious groups whose beliefs and practices that he disagreed with.

Theodosius allowed Christians to destroy pagan temples and in AD 391 he closed down all pagan temples and banned all forms of pagan worship.

They were also impressed by the way in which this new religion changed people's lives. In AD 324, the Emperor Constantine became a Christian. As a result, more and more important people became Christians. The Christian Emperor Theodosius banned other religions. The followers of Jesus were now members of the official religion of the Empire.

Pieces of silver from Water Newton, England, 4th century AD.

4.1 The Empire in Crisis

From the 2nd century AD, the Roman Empire was facing problems. After the victory over Carthage it had seemed as if there were no limits to what the Romans could do. By AD 100, this view had changed. The barbarian lands were wild and large. The Roman army could not conquer them all. There had been revolts, against Roman rule, along the rivers Rhine and Danube. At home, rival emperors competed to be in charge of the Empire.

In AD 122, Emperor Hadrian ordered a wall to be built in Britain. It is still called **Hadrian's Wall**. It marked one edge of the Empire. Other boundaries, or **frontiers**, were built in Germany and in Africa. The Romans had realized that there were limits to what they could do. They could not rule the whole world.

Things got worse for the Roman government. The population was falling in the lands around the Mediterranean. This meant there were fewer people to join the army and to pay taxes. The population was falling for a number of reasons. Changes in the weather caused poor harvests. This meant less food for people. Plagues also killed many people.

During the 3rd century AD, trade over long distances began to collapse. It was no longer safe to travel. Law and order was breaking down. Tribes from outside the Empire raided the rich lands of the Romans. These tribes needed more land. They also wanted the luxury goods made by Roman craftspeople. For years they had traded with the Romans. Now the collapse of trade forced their leaders to steal the luxuries they desired.

A boat from Nydam in Denmark, 4th century AD. Boats like this may have carried pirates raiding the lands of the Roman Empire.

A **SOURCE**

The Roman fort of Portus Ardaoni (Portchester) England. This fort was built in about AD 275. It was one of many forts built along both sides of the English Channel. These forts protected the Roman provinces from barbarian pirates (Saxons) from modern Germany and Denmark. They were called the forts of the 'Saxon Shore'.

There were wars in the east with Persia. There were problems all along the frontiers of the Empire. Towns began to decline because there was less to buy and sell.

In AD 251, a German tribe – the **Goths** – killed an emperor. Other tribes invaded the province of Gaul. In AD 270, the province of Dacia was abandoned by Rome. It could no longer be defended against the barbarians. The Empire was beginning to fall apart.

D

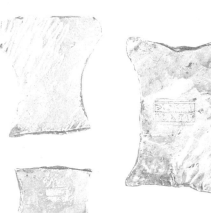

Hadrian

Hadrian (AD 76–138) was born in Spain, and was Emperor from AD 117–38. Under Emperor Trajan he was governor of Syria. He worked so well for Trajan, who had no sons of his own, that he was adopted as Trajan's heir in AD 117.

When he became Emperor, Hadrian toured the frontier provinces of the Empire to see if he could think of ways of improving their defences. From AD 120–21 he was in Gaul and along the Rhine frontier, living with the frontier legions. He then travelled on to Britain where he ordered the building of a wall to defend the north of Britain from tribes outside Roman control. This is the famous Hadrian's Wall, which separates England from Scotland today. He built a similar wall in Germany.

In AD 123 Hadrian travelled to the provinces of Asia and Greece, again to check the defences of the Empire. He then returned to Rome. In AD 128 he was in North Africa. He hoped, by constant watchfulness, to provide the Empire with peace and stability and to keep the frontiers defended.

Pieces of silver from Balline, Northern Ireland. They are stamped with an official Roman mark. They were probably paid to a barbarian tribe to stop them from raiding Roman provinces.

4.2 The Collapse of the Empire

To face the growing problems of the Empire, the army was reorganized. Some troops were kept along the edges of the Empire. Others were made into what is called a **field army**. This could be rushed to wherever there was trouble. However, there were not enough citizens volunteering to join the army any more. People were made to join. This is called **conscription**.

The Emperor Probus (emperor AD 276–82) began to encourage large numbers of friendly barbarians to join the army. They would then fight for Rome against other barbarians. Eventually, by the early years of the 5th century, whole barbarian tribes were allowed to move into the Empire, if they would help to defend it. These soldiers were called **foederati**. Sometimes they could not be trusted.

It was hard to run the huge Empire. In AD 285, Emperor Diocletian split the Empire into two parts. Two emperors (called **Augusti**) would rule. One would be in charge of the west of the Empire, one in charge of the east. In AD 293, each of the Augusti was given a helper, called a **Caesar**. Historians call this the **Tetrarchy** or 'rule of four people'. Even this did not help. There was still rivalry between emperors. The Empire suffered more civil wars as Romans fought Romans.

On top of these problems, prices were going up. This is called **inflation**. Money became worth less and less. In AD 301, Emperor Diocletian tried to stop the prices going up, but he failed.

Within the Empire, the population kept falling. Taxes went up as there were fewer people to pay for its defence. As parts of the Empire were taken by the barbarians, there were even fewer citizens left to tax. Taxes went up again.

In AD 378, more Goths invaded the Empire. They killed Emperor Valens at the **Battle of Adrianople**, in modern Bulgaria. They were being pushed, from behind, by an even fiercer tribe, called the **Huns**. In AD 406, other barbarian tribes invaded Roman Gaul. Some, called **Vandals**, reached as far as Spain and north Africa. Rome was now cut off from its source of grain.

A

SOURCE

The Roman General Stilicho, who was a barbarian; a Vandal. Like many barbarians, he fought for the Empire against other barbarians. He was executed in AD 408 because he failed to stop the barbarian invasion of Gaul.

B Should the Romans, as sensible men, have trusted the defence of Rome to gods who could not defend themselves? The only possible cause of Rome's destruction was this choice of such weak defenders.

SOURCE

The Christian writer Augustine, who lived from AD 354–430.

A mosaic from north Africa, from about AD 490. It shows a Vandal chief riding out from a captured Roman villa.

The Empire was falling apart. Many of the Roman provinces were lost to the barbarians. In AD 410, Alaric, a Goth chief, captured Rome itself. The Goths moved on from Italy, and set up a kingdom in southern Gaul. In AD 476, the last Roman emperor was overthrown by a barbarian chief named Odoacer. The western half of the Roman Empire had collapsed. Only the eastern half was left.

The barbarian invaders of the Roman Empire in the 5th century.

Stilicho

Stilicho (?–AD 408) was a Vandal warrior who fought on the side of the western Roman Empire. At first he was simply a mercenary, but he rose to become a powerful ruler within the Empire in the late fourth and early fifth centuries AD.

As he became more powerful, Stilicho took even more power. In AD 395 he had the chief adviser of the eastern Emperor executed. From AD 395–408, he was the unofficial ruler of the western half of the Empire, which was under tremendous pressure from barbarian tribes.

Stilicho fought the Visigoths in Greece (AD 395–97) and Italy (AD 402–3). In AD 405 he defeated an army of Ostrogoths who had invaded Italy. He was executed on the orders of the western Emperor Honorius.

Goths
Angles, Saxons, Jutes, Frisians
Huns
Franks
Vandals
Scots
Burgundians
Berber Desert tribes
Frontier of the Roman Empire

0 ___ 1000 km
0 ___ 600 miles

4.3 The Collapse of the Empire: Gaul

The Roman province of Gaul was made up of what is now France, Belgium and parts of Germany. As the Roman Empire got weaker, Gaul was invaded by a number of barbarian tribes. We know about these invasions from the writings of Roman historians, church leaders and landowners.

In AD 350, a tribe called the **Franks** crossed the frontier of the river Rhine and invaded north-eastern Gaul. They were looking for new homes. The rich Roman villas offered them a better way of life, if they could capture them. They destroyed 40 towns. They also took land and settled down inside the Empire.

In AD 406, more barbarians invaded Gaul. These tribes included the **Vandals**. They caused terrible destruction in Gaul. Soon Roman Gaul was split up into a number of little kingdoms. Each kingdom was ruled by a barbarian tribe.

The damage to Gaul was made worse by poor farmers who joined in with the barbarian tribes. These farmers were Roman citizens, but they were tired of paying high taxes to the Roman government. They wanted to get rid of their rich landlords and stop paying taxes. These poor farmers, who joined the barbarians, were known as **bacaudae**.

Modern archaeologists and historians are no longer sure that the barbarians were as destructive as some Roman writers tell us. Although the Franks were fierce warriors, they agreed to serve the Roman government. In AD 406, they fought the invading Vandals on behalf of the Roman government.

In time the Franks grew tired of serving the Romans. Under their chief, Clovis, they took more land for themselves. Soon Clovis had united all the Franks under his control.

The Franks were keen to take the best that Gaul had to offer. They wanted to live like wealthy Romans. There is a lot of evidence which suggests that they did not kill the Roman citizens of Gaul. The Franks even learned to speak a kind of Latin (the official language of the western Empire). Clovis himself even became a Christian.

A Death, sorrow, downfall, destruction, fire, unhappiness.

Lines from a poem written in the early 5th century AD. It describes the destruction of Gaul by barbarians.

B SOURCE At the end of the Roman period a number of villas continued to exist and evolved gradually as the centres of villages.

J. Percival writing about Gaul in 'The Roman Villa', 1976.

C SOURCE Leontius [a Roman citizen of Gaul] owns three villas, two near Bordeaux, which produce corn and excellent fishing.

From a poem written in about AD 550.

D SOURCE Before the 5th century, all the grave goods [things buried with the dead] could be described as Roman. During the 6th century there were Frankish weapons and brooches. The natives were just buying whatever happened to be available and fashionable. Not everyone in France became a Frank.

C. Hills, describing a cemetery in Gaul in 'Blood of the British', 1986.

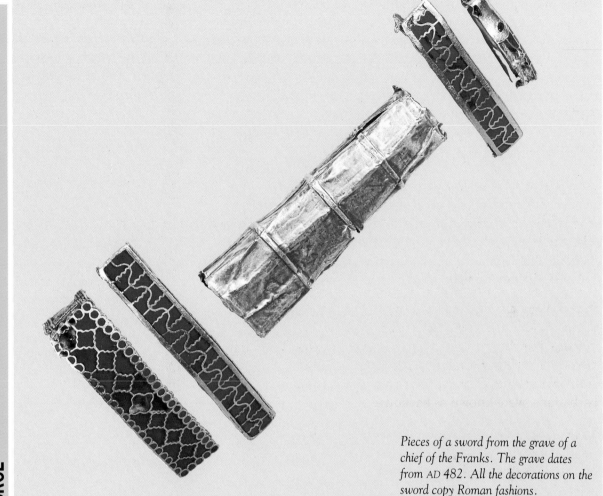

Pieces of a sword from the grave of a chief of the Franks. The grave dates from AD 482. All the decorations on the sword copy Roman fashions.

Clovis

Clovis (AD 466–511) was king of the Franks. He created the powerful Frankish kingdom in what is now northern France and Belgium. Most of what we know about him comes from the information that was recorded by the churchman Gregory of Tours towards the end of the sixth century AD. Clovis became king of the Salian Franks in AD 481. He conquered the Roman province of northern Gaul. To do this he had to defeat Syagrius, the last Roman ruler in Gaul.

Clovis married a Christian princess, Clotilda, from the barbarian kingdom of Burgundy, in AD 493. She tried to convert him to Christianity. In AD 496 he changed his religion and became a Christian, giving his support to the Catholic Church.

Clovis fought, and gained territories, in both the Rhineland and southern Gaul but the heart of his kingdom was in the north of the region, around what is now Paris.

4.4 The Collapse of the Empire: Britain

Britain was part of the western Empire. When Gaul was invaded by barbarians, the Roman government lost control of its provinces in the west. It stopped collecting taxes. After AD 410 no more coins were sent to Britain. Roman towns relied on trade and on taxes. When taxes stopped, the towns lost their reason to exist. The villas changed too. They had nowhere to sell their spare food. They did not need to grow a lot of food in order to sell it to pay taxes any more. They could no longer rely on skilled workers from the towns.

Until fairly recently, historians thought that the barbarian invaders of Britain took over Roman ways of life, as other barbarians did in Gaul, Italy and north Africa. Now it is thought that within about 30 years of AD 410, almost all the things that made Britain 'Roman', vanished. Towns were deserted, villas fell apart, the pottery industry stopped making pots.

As Britain became weaker, it was controlled by barbarians from outside the Empire. These barbarians were called **Angles** and **Saxons**. Before they came to Britain they had lived in modern Denmark, Germany and the Netherlands. Most of these newcomers arrived in Britain after AD 450. A few may have been here before this, as barbarian soldiers in the army. The parts of Britain which eventually came under the control of these barbarians came to be called **England**. These barbarians were the first English.

A SOURCE

◄ *Roman belt buckle worn by soldiers and government officials. This one was worn by an English warrior buried at Mucking, Essex, in about AD 400.*

B SOURCE

All the major towns were destroyed. A number of survivors were caught and killed. Others went to surrender to the enemy. They were fated to be slaves for ever.

Gildas, a British monk, describes what the English did to Britain in about AD 530. Gildas hated the English.

C SOURCE

1 AD 530. In this year Cerdic and Cynric took the Isle of Wight and killed a few men.
2 AD 530. In this year Cerdic and Cynric took the Isle of Wight and killed many men.

An English record of the victory of two English chiefs. The second account was changed later by an English monk.

D SOURCE

We can imagine Anglo-Saxon warriors storming the earthwork camps and stone cities, burning the towns and villas, slaughtering and driving away the Romanised Britons.

G. Trevelyan, 'History of England', 1926.

Historians once thought that the English came to Britain in huge numbers. This was because from the 5th century AD, people in eastern Britain began to be buried with English jewellery and pots and according to English beliefs. Also, the language of the English replaced the language spoken by the Roman Britons. It now seems more likely that the Roman Britons copied the fashions of their new rulers. This was largely because their own industries and ways of life had collapsed.

E

SOURCE

The number of Anglo-Saxon migrants to Britain was probably of the order of tens of thousands, as against an indigenous [native] population in the millions. It must mean active participation by large numbers of British in the Anglo-Saxon order of things.

A. Esmonde Cleary, 'The Ending of Roman Britain', 1989.

F

SOURCE

A pot made by a Roman British potter, but decorated with a shape and pattern popular with early English barbarians.

G

SOURCE

We cannot take it for granted that the Anglo-Saxon conquerors were so destructive as to expel, or exterminate, the Romano-British manpower.

M. Postan, 'The Medieval Society and Economy', 1978.

Gildas

Gildas 'the Wise' (AD 500?–72?) wrote one of the few pieces of written evidence which dates from the time when Roman Britain came under the control of the Anglo-Saxons. The book is called *On the Ruin of Britain*. It was probably written around AD 540. We do not know for certain who Gildas was, but he was most probably a monk at Glastonbury, Somerset.

Gildas believed that the Saxon invasions were a punishment visited on the country for the sins of the British. He described how a leader, named Ambrosius Aurelianus, led a counter attack against the Saxons which led to their defeat at the Battle of Badon Hill. After this the Britons had fallen out among themselves and were condemned by Gildas.

Some people identify Ambrosius Aurelianus as King Arthur, and say that Gildas' evidence proves that Arthur really existed.

4.5 Survival in the East

In the year AD 330, the Christian Emperor Constantine had a new capital city built for the eastern Empire. He built it on the site of a Greek town, called **Byzantium**. The new city was named after the Emperor himself and called **Constantinople**. It is now Istanbul, in Turkey.

When Rome fell, the eastern part of the Empire survived. Here, the Roman authorities kept control. Most people spoke Greek in this part of the Empire. In the western part, the official language was Latin.

Empress Theodora, Justinian's wife, gives a gift to an Italian church.

A

SOURCE

In the 6th century AD, the eastern Emperor Justinian tried to recapture the lost western Empire. In AD 554, he recaptured Rome and Italy from the barbarians. However, after Justinian died, it was lost again.

In the eastern Empire, the Roman way of life continued. Roman law was still obeyed. The Christian Church was very wealthy and important. Roman ways of planning and building survived. The eastern emperor was powerful. He ruled his Empire using a secret police called the **curiosi**.

In AD 1453, Constantinople was finally captured by the Muslims. Until that year, something of Roman life and government had survived in the eastern Empire.

C

SOURCE

By the end of the 6th century Italy was gone again. In eastern Europe too, Justinian had never been successful in dealing with the barbarians. The pressure from behind on these travelling people was too great, and besides they could see great prizes ahead. By Justinian's death a wedge of barbarian peoples separated west and east Rome.

J. Roberts, 'History of the World', 1980.

Justinian

Justinian (AD 482–565) became eastern Roman Emperor in AD 527. He was a great believer in the greatness of Rome, and hoped to regain the parts of the Empire which had been lost in the barbarian invasions.

Justinian recovered Africa from the Vandals in AD 533, then Italy from the Ostrogoths in AD 535–40. He then captured southern Spain from the Visigoths in AD 551. He fought off many attacks by the Persians.

Justinian reorganized the government of the parts of the Empire that were under his control, and reformed the laws. He was interested in buildings, and was responsible for many great buildings including the cathedral of St Sophia, which is still standing today.

B

SOURCE

Church of St Sophia, Constantinople. It was built on Justinian's orders and was first used for worship in AD 537.

4.6 The Importance of Rome

Hundreds of years after the end of the Roman Empire, people still remember it. The Romans amazed later peoples by their huge buildings, their careful planning of towns, the way in which they solved problems and their powerful army.

Many of these things were not invented by the Romans. Many of the 'Roman' art, carving and building skills had been inspired by the Etruscans and Greeks whom they conquered. Many of the Roman religious ideas came from Greece and the Middle East. There were not many entirely new Roman inventions.

What amazed later people was how the Romans spread ideas. The Roman Empire made it safe to travel. Skills and ideas spread as never before. Christianity became a 'world' religion because of the Roman Empire.

A

SOURCE

A group of Italian Fascists in the 1920s, dressed as Roman soldiers. At this time Italy was not a powerful country. These Italians were envious of countries, like Britain and France, which had empires of their own. They wished to make Italy powerful once more.

B

SOURCE

Painting of a Roman scene by the French artist Claude. He lived from 1600–1682.

The Romans showed that large areas could be controlled by one government. They also gave lots of different people a common identity. Although they had differences, these people were all members of the Empire.

Many people after the Romans tried to copy Roman planning and building. Many later laws copied the carefully-planned Roman laws. Later rulers tried to control many people, as the Romans had done. Even the Latin language is still used when something is given special importance.

D

British 50p coin. The letters 'D. G. REG' are a shortening of the Latin for 'By God's Grace: Queen'.

C

The Radcliffe Camera building in Oxford, England. It is the work of the architect James Gibbs, who lived from 1683–1754.

Mussolini

Benito Mussolini (1883–1945) was an Italian schoolteacher and a journalist. After the First World War, which lasted from 1914 to 1918, he started the Fascist Party in Italy.

In 1922 Mussolini took power and became dictator of Italy. He was impressed with the past greatness of Italy and hoped to build a new Roman Empire. He had a passion for order, and there was a standing joke that it was only under Mussolini, never before or since, that the trains in Italy ran on time.

In 1936 Mussolini conquered Abyssinia (Ethiopia). In 1939 he conquered Albania in south-eastern Europe. Mussolini was an ally of Hitler and entered the Second World War in 1940 on the side of Nazi Germany. He was overthrown in 1943 but saved by the Germans. In 1945 he was captured and shot and his 'empire' was defeated.

Actium, Battle of 26
Adrianople, Battle of 54
Africa 19, 20, 30, 31, 36, 42, 43, 44, 45, 47, 48, 52, 54, 55
Alaric 55
Angles 58, 59
Antonius Pius 39
Apollonius of Tyana 49
archaeologists 6
arches 40
Armenia 26
Arthur, King 59
Asia 18
Augusti 54
Augustus 26, 27, 28, 29, 48
Aulus Plautius 24, 25
auxiliaries 15

bacaudae 56
barbarians 30–31, 52–56, 58–61
basilica 38
Boudicca 32, 33
Britain 20, 22–5, 32, 52, 53, 58, 59
Byzantium 60

Caesar 54
Caligula 24, 27
canals 35
Carthage 12, 13, 18, 20, 52
Cartimandua 32
Cassius Dio 25
Cassivellaunus 22, 23
Cato 32
Christianity 29, 39, 50, 51, 56, 61, 62
Cicero 17, 28
citizens 15, 28, 30, 56
civil wars 26, 27, 54
Claudius 24, 25, 27
Cleopatra 20, 21, 26
Clovis 56, 57
Cogidubnus 47
coinage 11, 13, 16, 18, 26, 31, 36, 39, 54, 58, 63
colonia 28
Colosseum 41
Columnella 45
concrete 40
conscription 54
Constantine 39, 51, 60
Constantinople 38, 60, 61
consuls 16
countryside 44, 45
Cunliffe, Barry 37
curiosi 61

Dacia 53
Diocletian 54
Diodorus Siculus 22

Egypt 5, 20, 26, 37
entertainment 43
environment 4, 6, 10, 22, 23, 34, 35, 38, 41, 42, 44, 47, 52, 58

estates 44
Etruria 10, 62

Fabius Maximus 12
family 32–33
field army 54
Fiorelli, Giuseppe 7
foederati 54
Forum 17, 38
Franks 56, 57
freedmen 29

Gaul 10, 18, 20, 22, 24, 32, 37, 44, 47, 56, 58
gens 32
Gibbon, Edward 9
Gildas 58, 59
gladiators 43
Goths 53, 54, 55
Greece 10, 12, 14, 18, 28, 48, 60, 62

Hadrian 29, 52, 53
Hadrian's Wall 5, 52, 53
Hannibal 12
health 42, 52
Huns 54
hypocaust 46

inflation 54
insulae 42
Isidorus Hispalensis 23
itineraries 35

Jesus 50, 51
Josephus 14, 24
Julius Caesar 20, 21, 22, 23, 24, 26
Justinian 60, 61

languages in the Empire 4, 5, 30, 32, 56, 59, 60, 62
Latin 4, 32, 56, 60, 62
laws 28, 29, 63
legions 14
Livy 18, 19

magistrates 16
Maiden Castle 25
Mark Anthony 26
Martial 30
Masada 6
materfamilias 32
Maximus 12
Muslims 61
Mussolini, Benito 63

negotiatores 36, 37
Nero 27, 29, 50
numeri 15

Odoacer 55

paterfamilias 32
Paul of Tarus 29

Pax Romana 36
Persia 53
Petronius 28
plebeians 16
Pliny 35, 50
Plutarch 23, 34, 35
Pompeii 7
Pompey 20
Probus 54
Procopius 5
Pyrrhus 10

Republic 10, 16, 26
Roman
    army 10, 12, 14, 15, 18, 20, 22, 24, 26, 28, 29, 30, 31, 36, 52, 54, 62
    beliefs 4, 10, 11, 18, 26, 32, 48, 54, 62
    building skills 40, 41, 47, 58, 61, 62
    roads 34, 35, 36
    ships 34, 35, 36

Romulus and Remus 10, 11
Rubicon, river 20

Saxons 53, 58, 59
senate 16, 18, 20, 26
senators 16
Sicily 12
slaves 29, 46, 47, 58
Solinus 23
Spain 12, 20, 54
Spartacus 43
Stilicho 55
Suetonius Tranquillus 23, 25
Sulla 20

Tacitus 15, 22, 31, 50
taxes 28, 34, 40, 45, 52, 54, 56, 58
tenants 44
Tetrarchy 54
Theodosius 51
Tiberius 26, 27
towns 38, 39, 40, 41, 42, 44, 46, 56, 58, 62
trade 12, 13, 23, 34, 35, 36, 37, 39, 45, 47, 52, 54, 58, 59
Trajan 15, 35
transport 34, 35–6
tribunes 16
Twelve Tables, The 16

Valens 54
Vandals 54, 55, 56
Varro 11
Vespasian 24, 25, 27, 41
villas 46, 47, 50, 51, 55, 56, 58
Virgil 18

women 4, 16, 20, 30, 32, 33, 44, 60

Zama, Battle of 12